D0676828

JANE ADDAMS OF HULL-HOUSE

JANE ADDAMS
of HULL-HOUSE

A BIOGRAPHY WRITTEN BY

Winifred E. Wise

HARCOURT, BRACE & WORLD, INC.
NEW YORK

To my mother and my grandmother,
the one Jennie, the other Jane.

The author, Miss Winifred

E. Wise, has had my permission to use such material as she has

selected from my published books and articles, from my ~~Seminary~~ *College*

essays and orations, from letters written during my European

travels(1883-5, 1887-8), and from interviews with me.

Jane Addams

This volume, written for young people, is published.

with my consent,

Jane Addams

Hull House
Chicago.

CONTENTS

CONTENTS

JANE ADDAMS OF HULL-HOUSE

1

THE NEW HOME IN ILLINOIS

SARAH ADDAMS looked over at her worried young husband, John Addams, and gave a rueful glance to her fashionable new sprigged muslin dress and dainty slippers, now splattered with mud. The two horses hitched to the light carriage were snorting and tugging, but the wheels only sank deeper into the swampy mire.

"Halloo, strangers, need help?" shouted a brawny Irishman, wading through the muck. He lifted Sarah from the vehicle and carried her, hoop skirts and all, in his stout arms to the plank walk which was high and dry on stilts.

"Well, jus' phwat d'ye think iv Chicago?" he asked jovially. "They say it's to be gr-reat town."

Pushing together, the Irishman and John Addams

3

worked the carriage out of the slough and drove to firm ground on this main street of Chicago. Sarah climbed aboard, John Addams waved to the friendly Chicagoan, flicked at the horses with his whip, and turned their heads toward the northwest, avoiding stray cows, and mud-holes marked "This Way to China."

As the newly married couple rode away from the slab shacks and stores and out onto the Illinois prairies, they met wagons loaded with wheat and corn, driven by blue-shirted teamsters rough and heavy as the wagons themselves. Sometimes they turned out in alarm when two of these wagons raced towards them, neck and neck, the drivers standing up and lashing furiously. With the moon shining like a silver dollar in the sky, Sarah and John Addams stopped at a stage-coach inn and tumbled wearily to sleep in a big feather bed.

Before dawn, the bugle for the stage awakened them, and they dressed, breakfasted with other travelers, and went on again. That day they passed prairie schooners lumbering westward with kettles and pots dangling from the axles and with "women, guns, rifles, boys, girls, babies, and other nicknacks" peeping out from the canvas covers. Wherever a stream crossed the road, there were a sawmill and a cluster of log cabins and barns. Late in the afternoon of the third day, they saw in the blue distance the village of Freeport and pressed on eagerly. Soon they were driving past the Stephenson County courthouse and the general stores to the tavern where lead miners gambled and drank. This was Freeport in the summer of 1844, only eight years after its first settlement.

While Sarah rested after their long journey by Hudson River, Erie Canal, Great Lakes, and by carriage from Pennsylvania, John Addams searched the countryside for a home and business site. A place on the Rock River attracted him, but he finally decided on the village of Cedarville, six miles northwest of Freeport. With three thousand dollars—his total capital—he shortly bought the flouring mill on Cedar Creek. Twenty-two-year-old John Addams reasoned shrewdly that the land about Cedarville was rich—the fat kernels of the wheat and corn proved this—and that a flouring mill would make him money; he knew the trade. Besides, the wooded hills and rocky ledges of this peaceful hamlet reminded the young man of his native Pennsylvania.

Sarah was pleased too, when she saw the beauties and the promise of this spot, and with happiness and hope she moved into a log cabin near the mill and the water rushing over the dam. So ended the wedding journey of these two and so began the fruitful years in which nine children were to be born to them, of whom the eighth was to be Jane.

Soon it was clear that John Addams would be a leader in community life and thought. With several other men he started a village library, but bought few books "of a character which entertains without improving." These volumes were placed on shelves in the Addams home and circulated freely. That same year of 1846, he and enterprising others saw to it that the old log schoolhouse was replaced by a new building, over near the burying ground. Within the twelve-month, his interests were to range farther; he just had enlarged his mill and now felt more strongly than ever that his fortunes were those of the community.

A railroad was the talk at every cross-roads in Stephenson County; the farmers said they must have one to market their crops. Now, if they wagoned pork and grain to Chicago or over to the lead country near the Mississippi, they were lucky to get enough money back for traveling expenses. Merchants and mill owners agreed, and planned for an onrush of settlers should the "iron horse" reach Freeport. Shortly, John Addams and other interested citizens promoted a railroad convention at Rockford where Chicago financiers agreed that the Galena and Chicago Union line would run Freeport-way—if twenty thousand dollars' worth of the stock could be sold in Stephenson County.

Traveling from farm to village, public-spirited men like John Addams found women ready to buy shares with their butter-and-egg dollars and men with the money saved for a new barn. Though cash was so scarce that more than one youth had to exchange 'coon skins for a marriage license, the twenty thousand dollars were at last scraped together. And then—railway officials decided that the tracks were *not* coming to Freeport! But John Addams had a level head on his young shoulders; he and the older promoters got Rockford on their side and won.

"Hurrah for Stephenson! Let the cars come!" cheered a local newspaper.

The cars came in 1853. Next year, the grateful people elected John Addams State Senator on the Whig ticket.

Sarah Addams looked proudly at her tall husband whose serious gray-blue eyes, fringe of whiskers, and dignified walk made him look older than thirty-two. He was, to be sure, a State Senator and the owner of a flouring mill, a sawmill, and a farm. And she persuaded him to get a new blue broadcloth suit and high silk-plush hat fitting for a man of affairs.

Between legislative sessions down at Springfield, John Addams tended industriously to his business and continued to prosper. Whenever a farmer came back complaining that the flour ground for him in John Addams' mill was not the best and that his wife could not bake good bread, John Addams took a sample of the meal home to Sarah. After she had baked a crusty, close-grained loaf, her husband showed it to the farmer to prove that the fault lay not with the flour. He was too tactful to say that, perhaps, the other's wife was not as good a cook as Sarah.

With four youngsters in the family, the Addamses now needed a larger house; so they built a friendly brick home of ten rooms among the trees on the slope above Cedar Creek and the mills. The bricks and the wooden shutters were painted gray. Red glass was set around the front door, in Pennsylvania fashion, and a spindled stairway led up to a sitting room on the second floor, also a Pennsylvania custom. Usually the Addamses had so many guests at meals that the walnut table had to be set diagonally across the dining room.

The hospitality of Sarah and John Addams, their thrift and industry, were characteristic of the Pennsylvania Dutch (or, more properly, Pennsylvania Germans) among whom their forebears had lived. John Addams, however, was of English origin and traced his ancestry back to Robert Addams, son of an Oxfordshire squire, who had crossed the ocean with William Penn on his second voyage, late in the seventeenth century. No Quaker, Robert Addams had been a member of the Church of England, but he had admired Penn's fair dealings with the Indians and bought land from him near the new town of Philadelphia. Descendants of

Robert Addams had fought in the American Revolution and for generations farmed in eastern Pennsylvania.

One of the ten children of Samuel and Catherine Huy Addams, John Addams had been born in 1822 at Sinking Spring not far from Reading. He had gone to the common school and local academy and worked on his father's farm before being apprenticed to Enos Reiff, a rich Quaker miller over Philadelphia way. Here young John Huy Addams had taken the early turn at the flouring mill, starting work at three A.M., and here in his odd hours he had read through the solid books of the entire village library. His Quaker mother had early shared with him her ideals of "plain living and high thinking."

Soon he had been courting fine-featured, vigorous Sarah Weber, five years his senior; she had come from the Lehigh Valley for a visit with her sister Elizabeth, the miller's wife. A daughter of well-to-do Colonel George Weber, of Dutch descent, Sarah had had "advantages"; she had been to boarding school and was well-read, well-poised. After John married her in 1844, he had felt that he could better their fortunes in the

West. Courageously his bride had turned her back on the trim towns, the bursting barns, and the flowering orchards of the Pennsylvania she had always known and had come with him to a part of Illinois that was almost pioneer.

In the ten years since Sarah and John Addams had settled in Cedarville, the village had spread long and narrow so that each home could have gardens and an orchard. Four hundred people lived here now, among them so many Pennsylvania Dutch that it was a new Pennsylvania. The rose bushes and peonies, the bedspreads woven by hand in brilliant reds and blues, the home-spun linens, and the generous eating customs—all had been brought from Pennsylvania. The nurse of Sarah's childhood, old Polly Behr, was here to raise the Addams children, and James H. Addams, brother of John, had bought a farm and was rearing a numerous family. Farther to the south, near Sterling, Colonel Weber had built a mill on the Rock River.

Like many another freedom-loving Northerner, John Addams disliked slavery and did what he could to help the escaping negroes. Many a runaway black found shelter in the Cedarville home until he could be smuggled on toward Canada and liberty by the spring houses, barns, and basements which were the secret stations of the "underground railway."

Down at Springfield, Senator Addams had come to know and greatly to admire Abraham Lincoln, who was then practicing law but had already started to battle against the spread of slavery. So John Addams was no less eager than his wife and the excited children crammed in the back of the springy new carry-all as he drove into Freeport on August 27, 1858. It was the day of the second Lincoln-Douglas debate, a part of the "stump-speaking" campaign of Abraham Lincoln and Stephen A. Douglas in the race for the United States Senate.

Since early morning, the roads had been jammed with people on horseback, mule-back, ox-back, in lumber wagons and carriages, or afoot, hurrying into town. "All Prairiedom has broken loose," reported a New York newspaper. In courthouse square, three beeves were being roasted over a fiery ditch for the hungry crowd of men and barefoot boys, poke-bonneted

women, and girls in white pantalettes who had left home
before breakfast. When "Honest Abe" and "The Little
Giant" appeared together on the balcony of the new
Brewster House, they were cheered to the skies. Beside
smiling little Douglas, pompous in ruffled shirt and dark
blue coat, stood Lincoln, sad-faced and tall, wearing an
old stove-pipe hat and trousers that bagged at the knees.

Lincoln was thinking of the question he was going to
ask Douglas, a question that would embarrass "The
Little Giant." He was going to ask him whether a territory could keep out slavery. If Douglas answered
"Yes," he would lose friends in the South and his chance
to be President. If his reply were "No," he would dis-
own his child, the Kansas-Nebraska Act, and wouldn't
have a chance to be reëlected Senator from Illinois.

Lincoln journeyed out to the debating grove in a
prairie schooner, and, when the time came, he put his
poser to Douglas. "The Little Giant" flinched but then
replied in substance, "Yes, a territory can keep out
slavery."

When Douglas was elected Senator, Lincoln said that
losing out made him feel like the boy who stubbed his

toe—"it hurt too bad to laugh, and he was too big to cry." Yet the debates made Lincoln the talk of the nation, and some spoke of him as a vote-getting candidate for President of the United States.

After the Freeport debate, some claimed that, while the two campaigners were standing on the platform, Douglas, barely five feet tall, had looked up at Lincoln's six feet four and joked, "How long, O Lord, how long?" And that Lincoln had replied dryly, "The days of the wicked are short."

Another story, told for years afterwards by John Addams, was about a Democratic wag who went up to Lincoln and said, "Mr. Lincoln, I'm considered the homeliest man in Stephenson County, and yet I've been told I look like you."

Lincoln stared the man in the eyes and drawled, "Maybe so, maybe so. But I don't think I have quite so much cheek as you have. Not quite so much cheek."

2

THEY NAMED HER LAURA JANE

ORCHARD trees up the hillside were yellow with
harvest apples when another girl was born to
Sarah Addams on September 6, 1860, two years after
the Freeport debate. The downstairs bedroom was
quietly beautiful that morning with the sun coming
through the white curtains and shining on the four
circles, one within the other, carved on the low head
of the curving walnut bed. Old nurse Polly took the
baby and dressed her in clothes from the marble-topped
mahogany bureau, whose mirror swung between sup-
ports that tapered upward like church spires. The girl
child had her father's clear, gray-blue eyes and looked
as much like him as a new baby could.

A few weeks later, the infant was lifted from a home-made walnut cradle, in which her brother and sisters also had been rocked, and christened Laura Jane Addams. She was named after Mrs. Laura Jane Forbes, an intelligent young woman who had taught private school in the village before she married Colonel H. C. Forbes. Soon the other children were calling their little sister "Jenny"; for most "Janes" were "Jennys" then, so soon after the gala concert tour of Jenny Lind, "The Swedish Nightingale." The world was to know her in after years as Jane Addams of Hull-House.

Jenny was two years old and still sleeping in a little spindle bed when her mother died one winter day, giving birth to a child that did not live. The sorrow of John Addams and his family was the sorrow of the whole countryside, for Sarah Addams had been greatly loved. Always she had been the first to visit the bedside of the sick, rich or poor, bringing with her baskets of dainties, and bottles of quinine that might drive out the ague and fever.

After the mother's death, Mary Addams tenderly cared for the younger children. She was seventeen, and next to her was Martha, aged thirteen. From Martha, the children stepped down to jolly ten-year-old Weber, Alice, aged nine, and Jenny, the baby of the family. Four of the Addams children had died as infants. Capable far beyond her years, Mary ran the home with the help of old nurse Polly, a hired girl, a man-of-all-work, and a washerwoman.

When John Addams went to Springfield for the state legislature, Mary wrote him often concerning her charges. They all were well, she reported, though scarlet fever was about. Jenny wanted to know when her thumb would grow as long as her other fingers, and sent love and kisses.

A later letter from Mary to her father carried the grave news that Jenny was ill with typhoid fever. This, followed by tuberculosis of the spine, left her curly brown hair straight and her back crooked. She was pale and thin throughout her girlhood and held her head slightly to one side.

The frail child adored her tall busy father so much that she wanted to copy him. By the hour she sat in the mill, rubbing meal between her fingers, vainly trying to achieve a flattened right thumb, a miller's thumb, like her father's. When the miller was chiseling the millstone grooves sharp, she eagerly held out her tiny hands in the hope that the shower of chips would leave red and purple spots. Her father had these specks upon his hands from the years when he had ground millstones, but she couldn't get them, hard as she tried.

Down the village street, in the valley below the schoolhouse, bugles were calling young men to train for war, the Civil War, which now had been fought for nearly four bloody years. Across from this parade ground, the storekeeper's daughter watched the soldiers while she sewed on a quilt for her hope chest. Now and then a boy in blue came over and begged to take some stitches.

"For luck," he would say. "Maybe I won't be coming back."

John Addams was urging men to enlist, and promising free flour to the widows and orphans. He did not go to fight himself, perhaps because of his Quaker tendencies, but he had equipped one hundred soldiers, the Addams Guard. Meanwhile, his mill was working night and day to send flour to the front. And then—General

Robert E. Lee signed the terms of the South's surrender to General Ulysses S. Grant and the Union.

Six days later, small Jenny went outside in the soft April morning and found the gate posts draped in black. Running back along the wooden walk to find out why, she saw her father in the study, his eyes red with tears.

"Papa, why are you crying?" asked the startled four-year-old.

"President Lincoln is dead. He was a noble man."

As Jenny Addams grew older, Abraham Lincoln became her idol, as he was her father's. Several pictures of this great man always hung in their home, and when one day her father showed his letters from Lincoln, she touched them reverently. All the letters began with, "My dear Double-D'ed Addams."

The little girl liked to be with her elders, and she took an especial fancy to Miss Sarah Blaisdell, one of Martha's teachers at Rockford Female Seminary. When Miss Blaisdell arrived for a visit, Jenny said almost at once, "If you've no bejections, I'll go to your room with you." And she trotted up the stairs, informing the teacher that she had given pennies from her bank to help buv a carpet for the Rockford chapel.

Jenny was glad Miss Blaisdell was not there to see when she had a tantrum on her sixth birthday, kicking and howling with rage until nurse Polly said, "Jenny, if you cry on your birthday, you'll cry every day until you are seven, and nobody will love you."

The child stopped her sobbing, but felt so ashamed and forlorn that at bedtime she went to her father.

"Papa, do you still love such a bad girl?"

"I always love you, Jenny, no matter what you do," he comforted her. "But try to hold your temper."

Jenny shared nearly all her childish troubles with her father. Sometimes at night she lay wakeful and worried over a lie she had told, fearing that she would die before she had confessed to her father, and go to that sinner's Hell of which her playmates talked. When she could bear her sin alone no longer, she got up quietly—so as not to disturb Alice—and pattered barefoot down the carpeted stairs. At the bottom she paused, dreading to step on the clammy oilcloth in the hall and pass the unlocked front door. This nameless danger by, she hur-

ried through the blackness of the living room to her
father's bedside beyond and, awakening him, blurted
out the story of her wrong-doing.

Then, mind quite at ease, Jenny went bravely back
upstairs and slept soundly in the walnut bed with
peaches carved on its high back. She shared the room
with Alice, the room with one of its white-curtained
windows looking south at the stone storehouse and the
other window looking east over the moss-grown well
to the high barn with blobs of mortar holding the gray
stones together. Because they had no closet, Jenny and
Alice hung their clothes on hooks along the wall and
covered them with curtains. Often on chilly mornings
they had to break the ice in the water pitcher before
they could douse their faces. Teeth chattering, they ran
down to the large kitchen warmed by a Dutch oven.

That fall Jenny had started going to the red-brick
village school, down the road a way and up the hill.
With long brown hair held back by a metal hoop, she
trudged along in her blue gingham pinafore and copper-
toed boots, swinging her books from a strap in the autumn sun which yellowed the goldenrod and purpled

the wild asters. She sat with other small girls in the front of one of the school's three rooms, and from the first she was a good scholar. One morning, a boy across the aisle was wriggling his bare toes and looking out of the window when the teacher slapped his legs smartly with a ruler.

"Whatsa matter? I ain't doin' nothin'," protested the urchin.

"That's why I hit you," replied the schoolmaster.

Home from school, Jenny had her own tasks, set by her sister Mary. She cleaned the lamp chimneys and swept the front yard clean of needles and cones dropped by the tall pines along the wood-and-stone fence. Here no grass could be made to grow, and the earth was as bare and hard as a porch.

The October air was spiced with odors of apple butter being cooked in great iron kettles over fires near the Addams orchard. Round and round walked the man-of-all-work stirring the thick brown sweetness with long ladles, while the children begged him for samples or ran to taste the cider squirting from a mill on the barn floor. Already the best apples had been stored away in the

cellar for winter, along with potato and onion barrels
and crocks brim full of strawberry and raspberry preserves. Fat and unaware of Thanksgiving, the turkey
gobbler proudly spread his burnished tail.

Late in the winter, the gayety of sleigh-rides and taffy
pulls was ended by the death of Martha Addams at
Rockford of typhoid fever. She was a lovely girl of
sixteen, and had been called the prettiest of the Addams
sisters.

Jenny's first summer vacation from school was
troubled through its early weeks by a nightmare. Again
and again she dreamed that she was the only person left
alive and that she must make a wagon wheel to revive
the world. Even after the cheerful talk at breakfast, she
would remember and hurry down to the Cedarville
blacksmith shop to watch the smith at work and so prepare for her grave responsibility.

But she was not thinking about this bugaboo a few
weeks later when she was driving into Freeport with
her father. Gophers streaked across the road, and par-
tridges whirred out of thickets ahead of the carry-all
which had once carried the Addams family to the

Lincoln-Douglas debate. On the fences and trees, posters announced "the only Great Living Horseman" and "the facetious fiddlers," but this circus had been gone two days. It was enough for Jenny that she was on the way to town and could already see the factory smoke of Freeport which seemed to her a very large city with all its stores that sold crunchy peppermints and such pretty dolls.

That day they did not hitch the horses at the courthouse square, but drove directly to the mill at which Mr. Addams had business, down in "shanty town." Houses leaned tiredly against each other, wall paper peeled from the halls, and ragged little girls carried babies almost as big as themselves. This was Jenny's first glimpse of real poverty, and she whispered, "These houses aren't pretty like ours. They're ugly and so small. There's nowhere to play. Why do people live here, papa?"

"Because they have no money to live in better places," he replied.

Jenny wiggled her loose front tooth thoughtfully and then decided, "When I'm a grown-up lady, I'm going to live in a great big house, but I don't want it to be near other nice ones. I want to live right next door to poor people, and the children can play in my yard."

"That's a fine plan, Jenny," said her father. "I hope you *will* carry it out some day."

3

JENNY AND GEORGE

JENNY was nearly eight when her father married
Mrs. Anna Hostetter Haldeman, widow of a Freeport miller. She was a nervously brilliant woman, handsome and stylish, who had traveled and read widely.
Her older son Harry was studying in Europe, but young
George, Jenny's age, came with her to Cedarville. Little
Jenny was delighted to have a tousle-headed, brown-
eyed new brother as a playmate. To be sure, brother
Weber was always very kind, teaching her to skate and
fish, but he was grown up; he was sixteen. So, from the
first, Jenny was rarely seen without George or George
without Jenny.

Now that Jenny was so busy down at the mills with
George, the wax lady doll with yellow curls and open-

ing and closing eyes—still beautiful though her nose had
melted a trifle—fared no better than the prim china dolls.
Their mother seldom took them out of the pine cradle,
or served them tea at the little drop-leaf table. She much
preferred to ride logs daringly into the sawmill and
jump off just ahead of the screaming, big-toothed saw.
Or she and George would go to the flouring mill and
wet piles of bran for molding into pies and castles of
fantastic shape.

They were friendly with all the farmer boys who
rode to the mill astride plodding farm horses with bags
of grain flung across their broad backs. The miller
dumped this wheat or corn into a hopper from which
the kernels ran down between the round, grooved millstones and were crushed by the power of the creaking
water-wheel. While his grain was being ground and
sifted into flour, the farm boy went down to the mill-
race to try his luck at fishing. Jenny and George had
their hooks and lines too, and the three of them sat along
the bank. Sometimes a catfish tugged mightily, or a bass
slithered out on the grass. The fishing was better when
the creek was muddy from the rains, for if the water

were clear the fish could see too well and were too smart to bite.

Across the creek, limestone cliffs rose abruptly to a height of thirty feet with bushes and small trees climbing the crevices. Here was a cave that Jenny and George explored with a torch made from a cat-tail drenched in kerosene. Their shadows danced grotesquely on the spring-wet walls. Perhaps an Indian once had hidden here from his enemies, or perhaps they would step on a snake! Muddy and shivering, they came out into the warm sun.

When a rainbow banded the sky red, green, and yellow, the children rushed from the house to see whether an end rested on some place they knew, so that they could dig the pot of gold. Then the hired girl would call, "Jenny, you'll get freckles if the rain falls on your face while there's a rainbow."

But Jenny did not mind. She was a carefree, happy child who did not even wear a sunbonnet all the time, a lack which was reported as shocking by other children who had to veil their faces against sun and wind. In fact, like no other village girl, she also played knight, going on long crusades through the hills with George. The two knights-errant were tramping along the road one day when they saw a groom kiss his bride in a honeymoon carriage. The neighbors also witnessed this bold embrace and gossiped, "What *is* this world coming to?"

Tall for her age and thin, her head twisted a bit to one side, Jenny thought herself a very homely little girl. She did not know that her gray eyes were lovely, sometimes wistful and often merry, and that her smile was sweet. When strangers from the outside world visited the Union Sunday School in the spired Lutheran church, she could not bear to have them see that she was the child of her handsome father who taught a large adult class. On such Sundays, she did not walk home beside her father but trotted along with her cousins and her uncle James Addams. She told no one of these childish schemings but tucked them away for Sundays with the "Reward of Merit" cards earned for memorizing Bible verses.

One day in Freeport when she was on a main street, crowded with ladies elegant in sealskin cloaks and with whiskered gentlemen carrying canes, she quite unexpectedly met her father. He swept off his top hat and bowed low in humorous gallantry. So impressed was Jenny at this marked attention before all these fine folk that she never again was ashamed to let strangers know that she was John Addams' daughter.

Quite vain of a brand-new blue-and-white plaid wool cape with a blue velvet hood, eight-year-old Jenny dressed for Sunday School and came down to show her father.

"It's a very nice cape," he agreed. "But I wouldn't wear it to Sunday School and make other little girls who haven't new clothes feel unhappy."

Not too pleased, Jenny went back and put on her old cloak. As she walked along with her mittened hand in her father's, she was silent until the last corner when she said, "Some people have pretty clothes, and other folks shabby ones. Can't anybody *do* anything about it?"

"Perhaps not about clothes and such trivial things," he answered seriously. "That is why one should not try to outdress the rest at places like church and school where everyone can be equal in reverence and learning."

Of John Addams it was repeated that he never spoke

ill of anyone. If he could think of nothing good to say about a man, he kept still. So much respect did his opinions meet that many a villager and townsman said at election time, "I don't know how John Addams is going to vote, but I'm going to vote the way he does."

One wintry day, a farmer coming into the country store was told that his ears were frosted, but he insisted, "No, they ain't. 'Tain't cold. John Addams says 'tain't cold."

Now a man of property, John Addams owned, besides his flouring mill and sawmill, several farms along the road from Cedarville to Freeport. He was president of the Second National Bank in Freeport and a director of two insurance companies. Farmers living on the Cedarville-Freeport road claimed they could set their clocks by him, so regularly did he travel in to the bank on Wednesdays and Saturdays behind the white horses which he always drove.

Politically, he was a Republican State Senator. It had been suggested that he run for Congress, but he refused to campaign, saying, "If the people choose to elect me, I shall serve them."

Preachers, teachers, law-makers, soldiers, and other personages who came to the neighborhood usually hitched their horses at the Addams gate. Then Mrs. Addams brought from the built-in cupboard her fine white dishes, delicately traced with gold, and laid the table with handsome silver. Although the Addams home always had been hospitable, the second Mrs. Addams introduced a more elaborate social life and was known for her brilliant dinners and sparkling conversation.

After Sunday dinner, while the grown-ups were sitting at talk on the horsehair sofa and chairs in the upstairs parlor, Jenny and George played the tinkling German music box for visiting children and showed them around. They always stopped first in the hall below the chart of the Addams Guard which had the names of soldiers written below a brightly-colored battlefield and a sketch of Mount Vernon. Thoughts of the brave men who had dared their lives to free the slaves never failed to excite Jenny. Once, also, she listened to her father and "Uncle Dick" Oglesby, ex-governor of Illinois, discussing the bitter struggle between Union and Secession legislators in the War's early days. John Addams and other Unionists had hurried down to St. Louis to avoid the vote on secession or loyalty until the Union men had mustered strength.

Often the quiet of a country evening, when whip-poorwills called lonesomely and dogs barked far away, made Jenny think about all the sad things she knew—of a poor old couple, on a stump farm near the village, whose five boys had been killed in the War. Or she remembered her talks with Mrs. Clingman, widow of one of John Addams' first friends in Illinois. Sitting on the porch of her white house, the old lady told the eagerly listening children about her soldier son who had been brought home to die.

"Perhaps 'Old Abe' will get out and fly this way," Jenny and George told each other, watching the blue dish of the summer sky for a black spot that might be "Old Abe," the American bald eagle chained in the Wisconsin state capitol at Madison, eighty miles distant.

"Old Abe," as everybody knew, had been through the four years of the War with the Eighth Wisconsin Volunteers. Screaming, he had soared above the shots of battle but always had come back to his red-white-

and-blue perch. Whenever the regiment paraded, he had been carried beside the color-bearer, flapping his wings and whistling through his curved beak. Now, it was said, "Old Abe" attended more army reunions than either Sheridan or Sherman.

Though "Old Abe" never circled over Cedarville, the children—to their delighted surprise—were taken to see him on a carriage trip that lasted almost a week. He was just as they had pictured—big as a Thanksgiving turkey and with fiercely flashing eyes and long, sharp claws. But, as Jenny listened to the tales of his keeper, she looked past the bird across the white dome of the capitol. Somehow in this sweep, her child mind caught a sense of limitless space and of the limitless hopes of men. Somehow it suggested to her marching soldiers, and pioneers searching for homes across the prairies, and the nobility of Abraham Lincoln.

4

"IS MY HAIR WHITE?"

FAR down the side of a fifty-foot cliff, red-fringed with dancing columbines, was an owl's nest in the hollow of a scrubby tree that stuck out over Cedar Creek. Jenny and George knew it was an owl's nest because just at dusk they had watched the mother screech owl fly off to join her mate who was hooting news of fat field mice. Wanting to see whether eggs or owlets were in the hole, George decided to climb down and look. Carefully, he knotted a rope about his waist and wound the other end twice for safety around a maple near the cliff-edge.

"Hold onto the rope, Jenny, and don't let go," he warned as he started on his dangerous expedition.

Slowly he felt his way from one rocky ledge to the

next, gripping tough weeds and bushes. Suddenly a bowlder broke off, and he plunged down. Whipping away from the maple, the rope tore out of Jenny's hands. She stood there, and saw the sky, the tree, and the grass with dreadful clearness before she ran to the cliff-edge and peered over. There was George sprawled in the branches of the owl tree.

"Is my hair white?" he shouted up at her.

Strength Jenny might lack, but never courage. She recovered the rope-end and, bracing herself, held on with blistered hands while George crawled back up to the top. Scratched and bumped, he limped home beside Jenny, her hands wrapped in a handkerchief, to tell the shocked family about his narrow escape from breaking his bones and maybe his head.

To George and Jenny, mullein stalks rising above their blanket-velvet leaves in pastures looked like the feathers of Indian braves. Whooping, they slashed to right and left with wooden swords until every one of the imaginary warriors had been laid low. The placid cows gulped their cuds and looked at them with amazed brown eyes.

Walking over the meadows, shoes slippery from plant juices and thrust through with wisps of grass, the comrades surprised frogs which loped off on green-spotted legs. Whenever a garter snake tried to ooze away in an unseen S, George stepped on its tail with a yell, and they watched the forked red tongue dart out as it tried to tug loose its sleek, yellow-bellied body, fat with worms and young frogs. Sometimes they crushed the snake's head and carried it, still wriggling, between sticks to a stone altar they had built beside the creek. Here were the sun-dried skins and ribs of many a serpent they had killed, feeling perhaps in a dim, childish, half-savage way that these were sacrifices to the gods of nature that made the winds blow, the thunder roll, and the tiger-lilies red.

Far afield in their wanderings, these two heard the song of summer—crickets and grasshoppers fiddling merrily and locusts whirring in rising and falling cadence like the mowers in the hay. And they came to know what was good to eat in the moist woods—mellow May apples under green umbrellas, wild strawberries small and sweet, raspberries whose thorns caught at arms, and wild plums that burst on the ground and sent bees and butterflies staggering away drunk on the sun-ripe juice. But George and Jenny never ate the poison black berries of the nightshade nor the scarlet-stemmed, purple clusters of the Virginia creeper, so like the wild grapes that were good if one liked sour things. Sometimes the nettles stung red welts, or poison ivy raised itching blisters. They were always watchful for rattlesnakes, of which a few had been killed on the ledges and their rattles proudly displayed in the country stores by men whose accounts lost nothing in the telling.

In the smoke-blue haze of Indian summer, Jenny and George saw the golden pumpkins piled among the wig-wam-shocks of corn, and they climbed up to reach the hanging orange of mountain ash berries. Shuffling through drifts of red and yellow leaves to the shaggy hickories and close-barked butternuts and walnuts, they fought the scolding squirrels and came back with baskets spilling nuts to be dried on the attic floor. One day they bore to their creek-side altar three in every hundred of the nuts and poured over all an offering of autumn-gold cider. While several of their best-loved books were smoking to ashes on this ceremonial pile, they looked on gravely, the high-priest with a necklace of whitened snake-bones, the high-priestess with bracelets of the same.

When winter lay white upon the countryside, they found it hard to pull their sleds straight on the narrow path to school with the zigzag trails of rabbits to follow and the tracks of chickadees and weasels lacework upon the snow.

On February fourteenth, the mail brought frilly valentines for George and Jenny in white envelopes embossed with morning glories and forget-me-nots, colored by the sender's hand. As delicate as frost upon the windowpane, these valentines were white lace spun into shepherdesses, cupids, and love knots against orange and yellow tissue. Inside were sentiments:

"Forget-me-not."

And:

" 'Tis sweet to love, yet sweeter still
To be loved again,
But O how bitter is the thought
To love, yet love in vain."

39

This one was unsigned, but Jenny knew who sent it:

"When to ladyhood,
My friend, you grow,
Pray don't forget
Your little beau."

Spring made Jenny long for "after school" so that she and George could go to see whether the pink and purple cups of the hepaticas showed above their dead brown leaves. Home they would come with white Dutchman's breeches, yellow buttercups and cowslips, and frail anemones wilting in their hot hands, stained red with bloodroot.

On balmy evenings after supper, the Addams family often crossed the bridge and climbed Pine Hill. Here the wind sang through the Norway pines, planted from a bag of seeds John Addams had brought in 1844. They watched the sun set round and red, and stayed until the moon had brushed away the untidy rose and yellow scraps and set the neat stars in the purple sky. Back in the living room, Mrs. Addams sometimes strung her guitar from her neck with a black velvet ribbon and strummed an accompaniment to her cultivated soprano voice, singing old ballads like *Down By the Haunted Spring*. Bedtime came early to them all, for John Addams followed the habits of his youth, when he was a miller's apprentice, in "early to bed and early to rise."

Enviously, Jenny and the other children at school said that George and a girl named Anna Sill had "swallowed" the spelling-book, for these two always stood up longest in spelling bees. Tricky words like "lieutenant," "intelligible," "embarrassment," and "capillary" couldn't trip them. After the spell-down at Friday afternoon "exercises" came the nervous speaking of pieces— Lowell's *The Vision of Sir Launfal* with noble gestures, Holmes' *The Wonderful "One-Hoss Shay"* with pauses for laughter, and Whittier's *Snowbound* that started, "The sun that brief December day . . ."

Once a month the entertainment was climaxed by the reading of the school's newspaper from a long scroll elegantly festooned with ribbons. On this were copied in flourishing Spencerian hand the best essays, of high moral tone, and sly bits of gossip. Then the schoolmaster sounded "do-re-mi" on his pitchpipe, and the class swung into the words of *Tramp, Tramp, Tramp, the Boys Are Marching.* They closed the "exercises" singing *Just Before the Battle, Mother.*

Being such a man as is called "ahead of his times," John Addams on the school board insisted that well-trained teachers from the school at Normal be hired to instruct the children. Though these teachers had to be paid more than ordinary, they were able to give their students a better education than the "readin', writin', and 'rithmetic" of the usual village school and could even teach the older scholars Latin and algebra.

Jenny, her hair braided into pretzels now and tied with string, usually had her sentences parsed correctly or could bound almost any state north and south, east and west. She was even more clever at arithmetic but always was willing to help a friend do her problems.

If the teacher heard a girl scrunching parched sweet corn or if he caught a boy dipping a pigtail into a bottle of slate-washing water, he made them stay after school and write fifty times in their copy books, "Cedarville is a flourishing village."

At recess-bell, the boys whooped out on the school ground while the girls filed after, tying on knitted hoods and buttoning up jackets. The boys already were shooting marbles or flashing knives in mumblety-peg when the girls began to jump rope, showing their red flannel petticoats. Over in quiet corners, they traded plain and fancy buttons for their "charm strings"—the charm was having every button different. Or they exchanged bright-colored advertising cards from the Freeport stores, cards with dimpled baby faces on them, or girls feeding lambs, or lovers parting.

Tin buckets came out at noon, filled with lunches of mince pie, meat, bread, and apples, but Jenny and George lived close enough to walk home for dinner. That was why Jenny won a contest with Anna Sill one fall. They tried to see which could go longest into the cold weather without wrapping a scarf around her ears. Anna had to hike almost two miles to school, and so she lost.

When the air was soft upon their faces in the spring, the children loitered after school, sitting on the stones below Cedar Creek bridge and hearing the planks rattle overhead as a wagon passed. Here in the cool shadows they talked earnestly about how you were saved or you weren't, and went to Heaven or the other place in consequence. One girl, who had been to revival meetings, said you had to know certain words to open the gates of Heaven.

"You feel the Lord within you, and then you know what they are."

What were those mysterious words of salvation? Jenny thought they would *have* to be in the Bible and decided that, if you were to read the Holy Book quite through aloud, you would be *sure* to repeat them and so be saved.

And must you join a church to get to Heaven? Jenny stopped in the road and piled dust hills with her shoe, while she turned the question over in her mind. She just had heard the neighbor women hinting that the village doctor, who had died the day before, would not be saved because he had never belonged to a church. The doctor had been good and kind, that Jenny knew. If folk had no money to pay him, he cared for them just the same, her father said. Would not being a church-member keep

44

him out of Heaven? No. Her mind's eye saw St. Peter reading off such good deeds from his big golden book and saying to the doctor, "Enter."

Because praying in Latin seemed more holy, Jenny and George learned the Latin words of the Lord's Prayer and knelt every night, each beside his bed, chanting, "Pater noster, qui es in caelis; sanctificetur nomen tuum . . ."

5

GROWING UP

Perspiring in Sunday best, the good folk of town
and country lined up along Freeport streets, awaiting the Fourth of July parade. Here it came to the fifes'
tootle and the drums' rat-a-tat—Civil War veterans
marching in battle-faded uniforms, Mexican War soldiers, feeble survivors of the War of 1812, and red-
shirted firemen dragging an engine shined sun-bright.
The parade broke ranks at courthouse square, and
everyone jostled for elbowroom around the flag-draped
speakers' platform for the dedication of Soldiers' Monument. It had cost ten thousand dollars!

Ten-year-old Jenny, wearing white muslin trimmed
with blue ribbons, and George, in long trousers, were
sitting close in, big-eyed with pride as their father stood

up to unveil the monument and introduce the orator of
the day. He spoke well, did the Honorable John Addams, an upright man and a power in the community.
With a pull of ropes, he undraped the figure of "Victory," high above the courthouse elms atop a marble
shaft.

Later the crowd surged across the river to see a baseball game and a sham battle between Yankees and "rebs."
When the last skyrocket had blazed into the night,
horses were allowed to hurry away to the home oats.

Jenny and George knew every bump of the six miles
from Freeport to Cedarville. They had driven it so many
times—George in the front seat beside the hired man
and Jenny in the rear with her stepmother whose rus-
tling silks and flower-trimmed bonnets became her so
well. She always looked "like a million with interest,"
as the neighbors said.

With good roads, the trip took forty-five minutes;
with mud and ruts, an hour and a half. Black Hawk was
said to have farmed certain acres near by, and of him the
children often talked to shorten the journey. They
told each other how this old chieftain of the Sauk

and Fox had tried to drive white squatters from the Indian hunting grounds, how northern Illinois had rung with the screams of settlers, and how Black Hawk had been taken, a prisoner, to President Andrew Jackson. Jenny was glad all this warfare had ended twelve years before her father's coming to Illinois.

In Freeport, she ran off her scales for the piano teacher, trying to make the notes as separate as eggs in a basket. Sometimes she waited for her father at the bank until, stuffing business papers in his tall hat, he was ready to leave. With Jenny's hand tucked under his arm, he walked to the Pennsylvania House, where he kept his buggy in a livery stable that rented out chestnut horses for weddings and white horses for funerals. The hotel keeper hastened to put on his newest coat before he bustled out to greet the eminent John Addams.

When Alice Addams came home for summer vacations from Rockford Seminary, she brought jolly friends with her and stories about their crowd whose latest escapade had been floating a tub of stale butter down the Rock River so they wouldn't have to eat it. Though the Seminary suggested that a girl dress simply, it could not keep Alice's friends from letting curls fall over the right shoulder under pert little hats. Alice herself had her hair shingled and out of the way, but of course she had to be in style with long skirts and waists that fitted as though she had been "melted and poured in."

They all played croquet so far into dusk that they had to hold white handkerchiefs over the arches, and then they went into the house for games and fortune telling. Sometimes the Seminary girls slipped away to row romantically on the moon-velvet of the mill-pond with Weber's chums from the University of Michigan.

Almost as soon as he returned from Europe, Harry Haldeman, elder son of Mrs. Addams, fell in love with Alice Addams and she with him. A dashing young man, he played the piano with a careless brilliance that Jenny envied, and talked of student life and duels at the German university where he had been studying medicine. Everything seemed to amuse this Harry; even when the Cedarville barber missed the cuspidor and landed a tobacco cud on Harry's shirt, he laughed, "Go ahead, go ahead. Just keep on being sociable."

Mary Addams, who had been studying at Rockford,

49

was having her love affair too, with the Presbyterian minister, the Rev. John M. Linn. He courted the charming young woman so ardently that the neighbors joked, "She'll have to marry him to get rid of him."

But wed him Mary did, and a happy match it proved. They were married in the upstairs parlor before the white lace curtains of the bay window, with all the relatives there and Jenny sad at losing the sister who had mothered her.

About this time, the doctor ordered horseback riding for Jenny's twisted back; so a pony was bought for her. Side-saddle, she cantered up the lanes with the family's yellow dog, Ponto, trotting beside her. But the jogging pained her back so much that she hated riding. Had not the neighbor children raced the pony, he might have gotten fat from all the oats she gave him in the high barn where pigeons cooed on the log beams.

Every evening long before Christmas, after her stint of piano practice, Jenny sat under the hanging lamp close to the stove, embroidering cardboard picture-frames with yarn, pinking felt for penwipers, or crocheting napkin rings and chest protectors. Then she unwillingly started up to her icy bedroom carrying a hot flatiron to warm her feet. On Christmas Eve, she tied her hand-made gifts to the tree among white candles and festooned strings of cranberries and pop corn. Already the evergreen held presents for her that looked suspiciously like the ribbons and books she had been wanting.

Books the Addams home always had in plenty—sets of Dickens, Thackeray, Browning, Tennyson, and other great Victorian writers, bound magazines, geographies, and histories. Here, too, were still the volumes of the Cedarville library which folk came in to borrow. Books were everywhere—in cases along the living-room walls and behind glass doors above John Addams' roomy butternut desk in his office, near the Franklin stove that cozily opened up like a fireplace. One of the pigeon-holes in this desk, made by the village carpenter, was marked "The State of Illinois" and had held official stamps which Jenny never touched. Why, her fingers would have burned! Now, however, her father's sixteen years of public service as State Senator were ended, and all the stamps were Addams stamps.

Her adored father's stories of his early life as a miller's helper, when he had risen before dawn to read all the village library books, made Jenny want to know these same books so that, perhaps, she could begin to share his viewpoint on life. When translations of the *Odyssey* and *The Aeneid* seemed a little tiresome, she skipped on to a fat world history and felt very wise when it was finished. She also perused Plutarch's *Lives* and a long biography of George Washington. Reading and absorbing quickly, she made book reports to her father who encouraged her liking for history.

Cookery was as much to Jenny's taste as literature, and she baked a perfect loaf of bread in the year that she was twelve. John Addams had required this of all his girls; they were a miller's daughters and should know how to knead flour into food. Jenny's first loaf refused to rise, and her second looked as though mice had been gnawing holes in it. But at last her father cut through the crisp brown of one and approved; she had passed the test.

As a miller's daughter, Jenny knew well the anxious days of early spring when thaws and rains turned easy-

going Cedar Creek into an angry torrent. Down at the
mills, her father and his men labored with sand bags to
hold the dam against the buffetings of the flood. Trees
hurtled over the dam, and rocks and cakes of ice. And
then, more often than not, the structure gave way in a
dread crashing of timbers. Yellow waters swirled about
the mills and the millers' cottages, and horsemen gal-
loped to Freeport for masons and carpenters. The Addams home, being on high ground, was fairly safe.

Country girls were called in to help feed the men
working day and night to repair the dam, and a long
table and benches were set up in the huge Addams
kitchen which covered almost a third of the downstairs.
Here the laborers helped themselves to great roasts of
beef and pork, and cut thick wedges of spicy mince and
apple pie.

With the creek at last forced back into its bed, the
Addamses returned to their quiet daily round. At noon,
John Addams always went down to the store of Republican Mr. Ritchie (the Democrats traded with Democratic Mr. Benson) to wait while the mail was being
sorted. Here he settled in a snug chair beside the stove

with the spectacled cobbler, weather-beaten farmers, glib traveling men, and wandering preachers. They talked about the carpet-baggers in the South, the Chicago Fire, scandals of the Grant administration, the Franco-Prussian War, and whether it was time to plow. Their topics were, indeed, as various as the goods for sale in this general store. Bolts of merino, percale, and mattress ticking were piled up on shelves across from overalls, boots, "red flannels," and patent medicines. Groceries were weighed out at the rear counter, and harnesses and hay forks hung from the ceiling.

In summer, loungers sat on the store porch, whittling and chewing tobacco. John Addams never passed these barefoot boys and village prophets without a word or so. Though he had become well-to-do, he put on no airs and remained a neighbor to the country folk both rich and poor. So, first-hand, Jenny learned the true meaning of democracy.

At eighth grade, half a dozen sturdy boys left school to work in fields or stores, and many a girl stayed at home to mind the younger children and help with putting up eggs and putting down pickles, knitting mittens, and baking pie for breakfast. Only a handful continued on with Jenny and George, and these wished they hadn't; for algebra was hard and Latin a bugbear. Under his breath, someone was always grunting:

"Latin is a dead, dead language.
It killed all the Romans,
And now it's killing me."

Girls were doing up their hair in "waterfalls" now and putting willow whips in petticoat hems to make their braided cashmere dresses stand out. On Hallowe'en, they shrieked in mock terror at the unearthly groaning of "horse fiddles" under their windows when boys drew rosined boards across wooden boxes. If the class wag whispered around the schoolroom, "What sweetmeats did they have in the Ark?" and no girl could think, he would yell, "Preserved pairs."

Or he would catch them on another one. "How do you save a dying duck?"

The answer to this was, "Send for a quack doctor."

Jenny and quiet George were still as close as two fingers on one hand and, preferring to hike and read

together, usually did not mingle with their classmates
outside school hours. At school, however, Jenny had a
special prestige because she could read letters from her
sister Alice, now in Europe, about the crown jewels in
the Tower of London and the candles burning eternally
in St. Peter's.

Already Jenny was someone on whom the family de-
pended. When word came that nurse Polly was dying
in her cousin's farmhouse near by, she was driven
through a blizzard to her. Alone with the storm, Jenny
sat beside her dear old nurse, and she was alone when
the dying woman gasped, "Sarah," the name of Jenny's
mother. Polly was dead, and Jenny ran to call the cousins from the kitchen below, where they were having
supper.

Homeward through the white snow with sleigh bells
jingling, the girl felt warm and alive coming away from
the strangeness of death. What was death and what was
life, Jenny wondered, what was youth and what was
old age? She remembered her terror as a small child
when she saw clay thrown on the coffin of a school-
mate's mother and first realized that bodies were buried

in the gloomy earth. And she thought of her dead sister Martha. Perhaps Jenny's own frailness made her more reflective than most girls of fifteen.

That summer, satchels packed with their best clothes, Jenny and George set out with Mr. and Mrs. Addams for Philadelphia and the Centennial Exhibition, which celebrated the one hundredth birthday of American independence. It was the young people's first long train journey and their first acquaintance with Pullmans and diners. By hack or horse-car, they traveled every day from their aunt's house in Philadelphia to the Exhibition where the sight-seeing gave them blistered feet and mental indigestion.

Glass workers blew goblets, a Swiss clock chimed a different tune every hour, a sleeping lady and her couch were sculptured in butter, and looms wove Turkish rugs. Here were bowlders of gold and silver ore from Colorado, telegraphs and type-setting machines, steam engines, a handkerchief of linen spun by Queen Victoria, prize dogs and horses, diamonds and emeralds. It was so hot that washerwomen filled their tubs with lemonade to sell, and Philadelphia papers sarcastically suggested snow for frost-bite. More memorable to Jenny and George even than the Exhibition was their visit to old Independence Hall with the Liberty Bell and the plain old desk on which the Declaration of Independence had been signed.

Home to Cedarville they carried souvenirs and a portrait taken by one of the best photographers in Philadelphia, America's second city. Mrs. Addams stood behind George, who had his arms folded in manly fashion, and Jenny, who had her hair waved and wore a chain with a gold cross over her high fluted collar and lace jabot. The once awkward child was now a charming young girl with a beautifully shaped head and with large expressive eyes under daintily arched brows.

Alice Addams returned from Europe and, still in love with fascinating Harry, married him and went with him to his medical practice in Iowa. She took with her a supply of preserves and pickles canned by her devoted sister Jenny. Weber too was married and settled on a near-by farm stocked with pure-bred Jerseys. (Jenny had mumps and couldn't go to the wedding.)

Graduating from the village school, Jenny and

George were collecting autographs and writing in their classmates' plush albums. They tried to be a little more original than the usual sentiments, expressed in swirling T's and trilling M's, like:

"Twine one bud in Memory's Wreath for me."

And:

"As birds in prison cages
  Sing when other birds have fled,
  So the words on Album pages
  Speak, when Whispered words are Dead."

Like her three sisters before her, Jenny was headed for Rockford Seminary, of which John Addams was a trustee. She had hoped to go to Smith College, far away in Massachusetts, but her father preferred to have her at Rockford, "The Mount Holyoke of the West," only thirty miles from home. She would have a broad education, graduating there and then going abroad for a year or so.

Most people in the '70's believed that a girl who could write a beautiful hand, paint roses on china, play the piano gracefully, and read fluently was a very accomplished young lady. Why trouble her pretty head with higher education? Of *course* woman's place was in the home, in the parlor crocheting if she were rich, in the kitchen cooking if she were poor. But John Addams thought differently. He wanted his girls to be as well-educated as young men so that they could stand on their own feet and think independently. If they married, all right. If they chose careers—well, they would be ready for them.

At Springfield during the legislature, he had come to know eloquent, iron-willed Miss Susan B. Anthony and had championed her when other legislators ridiculed her battle for women's rights. A man "ahead of his times," John Addams believed that women should share equally with men in the affairs of the world.

6

A SEMINARY GIRL

WHEN Jenny arrived in Rockford with her tall father one golden September morning, she looked hard at the ivy-covered, weather-stained bricks of Rockford Seminary and wondered how she would like going to school there. Sturdy like the pioneers who built them, Middle Hall raised its white cupola and flagstaff above adjoining Chapel and Linden Halls with their friendly porches and square windowpanes.

So long was Jenny's good-by to her father that she was too late to get paper on which to write her entrance examinations. But another new girl, vivacious little Nora Frothingham, shared hers; and they walked into the classroom, scared as though they were children and not young ladies with dresses dusting the floor.

This first day they answered questions in arithmetic, grammar, geography, and algebra. Next day, they were sharply quizzed in Latin Grammar and Caesar, history, and zoölogy, guaranteed to houseclean the brain of whatever knowledge was left in that attic. The fifth zoölogy question—asking the difference between a dog and a cat paw—puzzled Jenny; she looked across the aisle at Nora and held up five fingers. Nora spread out her hand and then hooked the fingers back like cat claws, thus cleverly answering Jenny.

Newcomers who passed most of the tests were permitted to enroll in the Seminary, joining a student body of nearly two hundred girls. The yearly fee for board and tuition was one hundred and seventy-five dollars.

Asked if she were homesick, one freshman replied, "No, I'm not. I only wish I were somewhere else, and I think I'm going to die."

Just seventeen, Jenny almost echoed this before the strangeness wore off and she was settled in her high-ceilinged corner room on the second floor of Linden Hall. She had brought her own carpet to make the floor warmer for wintry mornings; the room was already furnished with a walnut bed, two study tables, a rocker, and shelves for schoolbooks and for the required "Bible, *Sabbath Hymn and Tune Book*, a dictionary, and standard poetic works." White sills of the tall windows were broad enough for sitting on and looking out over the flower beds and through elms to the picket fence at the rear of the campus, and beyond to the shimmering Rock River. A fireplace of glazed brown brick was closed up and fitted with a box stove.

As genteel exercises, Seminary girls were supposed to walk on the campus every day for an hour and to take gymnasium twice a week in loose blouses and ankle-length skirts. Arms folded across her chest, Jenny promenaded dutifully, but, because of her back, she did not take gymnasium. Much to her dismay, however, she had to ride horseback, as at home. The very first Saturday morning she found a horse saddled and ready by her father's order.

Up at seven, "lights out" at ten was the Seminary rule, but this often was defied when a girl opened a box from home. She hung blankets over the transom to keep the lights from a teacher's eye and invited her chums to a midnight "bum." Her little stove, roaring with kindling donated by the merrymakers, heated the room to 100° in the shade. Taffy boiled on the stove. Corn popped over one gas jet, and oysters stewed over the other. On such hilarious occasions, Jenny was skillful at frying eggs above a lamp in buttered boxes of paper, while another guest arranged sardines artistically in a soap dish. A third went upstairs to the chemistry laboratory to boil cocoa on a Bunsen burner, and the rest picked out nuts with new hairpins. Sometimes over-loud giggles brought a stern preceptress to order them all to their rooms, perhaps leaving half a chocolate cake behind.

Jenny and her roommate took turns getting up first in the morning to close the windows and light the fire. In zero weather, one freshman tried keeping her stove going all night with the windows shut and nearly turned into a "smoked ham." If the school misses did not have time to dress between the rising bell and breakfast, they slipped into flannel wrappers and hurried downstairs.

Like the other Seminary girls, Jenny and her friend dumped out the stove ashes every morning, swept their room, and carried their own wash water; but that didn't count toward the hour of "domestic duty" required of each student daily. A senior sat at the foot of every dining table and served, while the freshmen were always hopping up to re-fill the water glasses or bread plates; but even all this didn't count. "Domestic duty" was setting and clearing tables, washing glasses and silver, answering the door-bell, sorting mail, straightening up classrooms, making pies and cakes, and dusting. So, in 1877, the Seminary taught the girls womanly work and saved money.

When the cry, "Apple man, apple man," went round in the fall, half the school rushed out with pails and waste baskets to fill them with juicy winesaps and russets from the apple man's cart. Nobody could study without an apple to chew. And what was a "comb concert" unless one munched between selections?

With the ivy waving scarlet banners, a crowd would rent a horse and carriage on Saturday afternoons and tour Rockford, "The Forest City," which had many imposing homes with towers and fancy gables. Jenny often was invited out to supper by her father's Rockford friends, but she always had to be back at the Seminary for Sunday which was observed with earnest devotions.

Wednesday mornings were set aside for the arts, as no visitor could doubt who heard the soprano warblings and the piano grace-notes, or saw waterfalls and forests being painted in oils. Off-hours during the rest of the week, musicians practiced noisily in little rooms along the lower hall, and artists gilded coal shovels ready for garlands of red roses. If some unhappy girl simply could not sketch, she teased her roommate to decorate bits of satin with forget-me-nots and daisies. These she must have for the ends of a white mull necktie to wear on her dark school dress. Although Jenny painted, she preferred taxidermy, mounting squirrels and owls.

Shopping on Wednesday afternoons for side-laced boots, bonnets, and crochet patterns of slippers and match-box holders had to be modest, for every week a teacher went over each young person's account book and talked to her about extravagance or scolded her for wearing elaborate jewelry. But, for that matter, under-classmen weren't allowed to go downtown without a teacher to chaperon them in this fair-sized factory city; only seniors went about alone.

"Plain, inexpensive clothing, especially flannel; also wool hose and a pair of India rubber overshoes, a waterproof cloak, and an umbrella" were necessary, the school catalogue admitted, but called most other things luxuries. Each damsel was expected to bring from home her bedding, a fork and teaspoon, and table napkins. Some girls added a spice of variety with fringed red-and-white-checked ones.

Because one had to pay ten dollars extra a year for tea and coffee, most school misses drank water and milk instead. And they groaned about the meals—mutton Thursday noon, fish on Friday, chicken Sunday the year around—with few surprises for the hungry crowd that swarmed down the stairs to the cheerful, many-windowed basement dining room. One evening a girl up ahead spied a tempting yellow bowlful on the serving table.

"Floating island!" she whispered joyfully, and the word was passed back, "Floating island!" But a closer look showed it to be only corn-meal mush.

In round careful handwriting on lined paper, seventeen-year-old Jenny composed an English theme on

Unknown Quantities that her teacher marked "quite good":

"Whenever a king dies in Egypt a solemn tribunal sits as umpire, judging his worth, and giving or denying to her dead king the tomb of the kings. . . . They review his *deeds*, and his deeds alone: . . . all his aspirations, struggles and strivings are unknown quantities, they have nothing to do with them. . . .

"Thus man today sits as a solemn tribunal judging his fellow man, and giving him fame or infamy. . . .

" 'If it had not rained on the 18th of June 1815 the whole fortune of Europe would have been changed, a few drops of water more or less prostrated Napoleon.' Had the ground of Waterloo been dry and the artillery able to move at the proper moment, the entire scale of fortune would have been changed. . . . All historians acknowledge his plan of battle to be a masterpiece, and yet the people only know that Napoleon was beaten. . . .

"Thus the world and the mass of common people which is the voice of God, judge, not on what might have been if it had not rained, not on the motive or the effort put forth, but on solely what *is*, and in this dread opinion 'we are what we must, not what we would be.' "

Already this frail, clear-eyed girl saw the difference between dreams and deeds. She was preparing for a life of action.

In Latin class, Jenny (now more commonly called Jane) met brown-haired Ellen Gates Starr, a small, lively, intensely artistic person whose blue eyes often flashed in argument. Emotional Ellen, always close to laughter or tears, and calm Jane Addams were to be life-long friends.

Ellen made flowery Latin translations and wrote learned articles for the Rockford *Seminary Magazine* on such subjects as *Florence and Edinburgh* and *Soul Culture.*

"Ellen writes just like Ruskin," said her awed classmates.

Just before the Christmas holidays, certain favored Rockford youths were allowed to set up a tent in chapel for the bazaar. By noon the tent would seem ready to be festooned with evergreens and lined inside with tables displaying walnut candy, landscapes, beaded pin cushions, and hand-painted lemonade pitchers and cracker jars. Then something always happened, and the canvas would crash down. So the gentlemen had no choice but to remain all afternoon fussing with ropes and flaps. It was generous of them, surrounded as they were by girls admiring their strength and running up stepladders with a twinkle of striped hose to hang Christmas bells.

Beaux had to be properly endorsed by teachers or parents before they were allowed to call on the well-guarded misses. But the boys from Beloit College, brother to Rockford Seminary because it was founded at the same time, were admitted without such passports. On Class Days, these students drove the twenty miles from Beloit in full force singing:

"I looked down the river
  And what did I see,
  A-comin' for to carry me home,
  But a Seminary girl a-comin' after me,
  Comin' for to carry me home.
  She came so fast
  I fell on my knee,
  A-comin' for to carry me home.
  And prayed, 'Oh, Lord, have mercy on me.'
  A-comin' for to carry me home."

A steamboat trip on the Rock River was followed by an evening serenade. Always, before the Beloiters left, fresh initials were carved within hearts on the campus elms. George Haldeman was one of the Beloit band, and another was a handsome youth, later to be a noted scientist, who wouldn't have minded if Jane Addams *had* come "for to carry me home." Jane herself blushed pink as the roses he sent her when teased about him.

Few girls slept well on the night before Class Day, what with romantic thoughts and with fringes painfully done up in tea-lead and back hair in rags. In the morning they raced between bath tubs and mirrors, rubbing cheeks red with flannel, shaking out curls, and helping each other in the matter of hair-dressing and buttoning up the back. The most fashionable belles laced their waists tighter than ever by drawing the corset strings over bedposts, and plumped out the puffs of their bustles and the ruffles of their bosoms to show off their "hour-glass" figures. But Jane and her friends refused to torture their waists even for parties, and clung to coat dresses with simple, though modish, lines.

For week days everybody agreed that the waists of

fashion were too tight and the skirts too long. They wished that they could wear something more comfortable—the loose gymnasium costume perhaps. "The clothes we wear are bad for our health," said the wise ones, and all of them longed to throw aside the iron corsets and petticoats galore and be free. They were tired of looking like be-ribboned packages waiting to be called for.

The flowers that bloomed in the spring weren't called just trillium and anemone anymore by the schoolgirls, but *Trillium cernuum* and *Anemone quinquefolia*. Botanists in bustles were walking all over the woods now, picking flowers and plants and taking them home to press and classify for their herbariums. Jane and the others set out at six in the morning on one long expedition and came back at noon, much bedraggled, with hands full of *Taraxacum officinale* specimens (dandelions). They had fallen into a creek and tried to dry off over a bonfire. Sometimes their scientific interest led them to go "bugging" in a buggy, and once the school survived bread made in Jane's chemistry class.

During the summer, Jane and keen-eyed George

roamed the Cedarville country looking for strange plants, birds, and "lead blossom" and "sunflower coral" fossils in the rocks. George took his pencil too and sketched the mills, the dam, and other village scenes to make his herbarium truly artistic. He did things easily, and most very well.

As in their childhood, Jane and George were together again, free to ramble in sun and cloud, breathe the red clover, and see willows and alders fishing in the creek. But now it was not enough that they love the out-of-doors; they must examine all nature with scientific curiosity. They saw insects eat plants, birds eat insects, and cats eat birds, small dramas in the struggle for existence of all living things. And they knew that the leaf-green of the katydid and the thicket-brown of the partridge were examples of the protective coloration that helped the fittest to survive. It was Charles Darwin who had opened their eyes, Darwin who was revolutionary with these ideas on evolution and, more especially, with the theory that men are descended from some lower form of life.

Following Darwin, George kept fat angleworms in

pots for minute observation of these small plowmen of nature, so vastly important in the scheme of the universe. Such pure science as data on earthworms was too cold and abstract for Jane, and she honestly admitted that she never could be a genuine scientist like George. Still, she was so interested in Darwin's theory of evolution that she carried back to Rockford various scientific works owned by her stepbrother Harry, including Darwin's *On the Origin of Species* and *The Descent of Man.* It was thought quite daring, in the religious halls of Rockford, to believe in Darwinism, because it did not accept all the Old Testament as gospel. But Jane was not a rebel so much as a logical thinker, and she wanted to learn all she could about science in general because already she had made up her mind to be a doctor among the poor. Her own delicate health made Jane acutely sensitive to the sufferings of others, and she had, beside, grown up in the light of her father's ideals of public service.

7

"LET'S *SAY* SOMETHING"

ONCE again through the long autumn evenings began the schoolgirl "confabs" in the Seminary rooms. Were you happier when young, or was the best "yet to be," as Browning wrote in *Rabbi Ben Ezra?* Did you want fame, or would you be content with a white cottage full of rosy children? Were you going abroad as a missionary to teach brown-skinned natives, or were you going to stay at home and help the poor and luckless? And how could you do your small part in getting the vote for Woman, and better jobs and better education?

What were you worth? What should you do with your life? And what would life do to you?

It was Youth asking questions of the sun, moon, and

stars. It was Youth reaching out for life which seemed so far away from this sheltered dormitory.

One of these eager questioners who talked as hard as she studied was Catherine Waugh who was to be her husband's law partner in Chicago and work for women's rights; and another was Katherine Tanner, beautiful of face and figure, who would win fame as a concert singer. Annie Ellers, later a medical missionary and royal physician in Korea, was here, and so were Anna Sidwell, future teacher of the blind, and Nora Frothingham who was to start a school in Japan with her missionary husband. None gave forth more decided opinions than Ellen Starr who was to found Hull-House with Jane Addams. Because these young women were among the privileged few of their sex at this time to enjoy higher education, they felt perhaps more seriously than later generations of students a responsibility for making their lives worthy.

Close to hand was something they could work for immediately—helping change Rockford Seminary into Rockford College as part of the drive for Woman's college education. To this end, they persuaded the

Seminary to give courses in higher mathematics and Greek. Catherine Waugh and Jane, both of whom had logical minds, studied mathematics to fit themselves for bachelor degrees when the school should be allowed to grant them, and Jane was one of the few who took Greek under Miss Sarah Blaisdell, whom she had loved since childhood.

Jane was busy, too, selling advertising and being Home Items editor for the Rockford *Seminary Magazine*, a little quarterly with a gray-flecked cover whose subscription price was a dollar a year. If Maria Nutting, editor-in-chief, tried to change the wording of her articles, Jane always insisted, "But this *sounds* well, Nuttie."

Rarely excited or angry, never speaking ill of another person, Jane Addams was becoming one of the best-loved girls at the Seminary. She was a girl who really seemed to care more for others than for herself. When she asked, "How *are* you?" she really wanted to know. Though somewhat shy and quiet, she had a magnetic personality that drew people to her almost instinctively. Little did her schoolmates know of the pains which

often racked her back, but they all felt in her something of the high courage and determination she quoted
one morning in chapel, when writing on the flyleaf of
Nora Frothingham's hymnal:

> "Life's a burden, bear it.
> Life's a duty, dare it.
> Life's a thorn-crown; wear it
> And spurn to be a coward."

As junior class president, Jane was one of those
"called on the carpet" to confess who had disgraced the
Seminary at the annual Day of Prayer. A reverend
gathering of ministers and educators in chapel had suddenly started to sneeze and cough. Red pepper had been
scattered about by someone. A junior was suspected, but
no girl ever tattled.

Soon after, Jane and her classmates were planning a
triumph for the archery contest with the sophomores.
At every school event, the juniors had met audacious
competition from the sophomores, and so now they con-
spired to vanquish their rivals once and for all. Zealously
the third-year girls practiced shooting, and secretly they

had made for the contest broad-brimmed straw hats or-
namented with poppy red ribbons and festoons of wheat
ears. Their class flower was the poppy which grew
among the wheat in Europe; and their class motto was
hlaefdige, the Anglo-Saxon word for lady, which meant
"bread-giver" in translation.

On the April day of the tournament, the juniors
strutted around the archery field in their fetching head-
gear to the cheers of the crowd. But then—one giggle
swelled to uproarious laughter as the saucy sophomores
minced out mockingly wearing outlandish sunbonnets
in *their* colors of gold and cherry red.

"Who told? Who told the sophomores about our
hats?" The "Bread-Givers" buzzed so angrily that in
their indignation they overshot their targets and only
tied the sophomores.

Those impudent sophomores didn't know their places.
A few weeks later, on the evening before the Junior
Exhibition, they burlesqued the forthcoming display of
junior talent in learning and the arts. One second-year
girl, impersonating modest Jane Addams, was so bold
as to get up and sing-song:

"I am the president of this 'ere class,
I'm '81, I'm '81.
I am a most susceptible lass,
I'm '81, '81."

The whole school was still tittering the next night
when the Beloit gallants arrived and the Junior Exhibition opened with music. But even the sophomores had
to admit that Jane's junior oration on *Bellerophon* was
an extraordinary success—though they couldn't understand a word of it. She actually talked in Greek! Jane
had worked weeks on this speech, checking the grammar with the learned. Somewhat breathlessly at first, she
had drawn a parallel between Bellerophon's victory over
the monster Chimera—while mounted on the winged
horse Pegasus—and the winged idealism which alone
can conquer social wrongs. It was common for a young
woman to choose her lofty theme from Greek myth,
but not for one to speak that ancient language nor to
give such vivid prophecy of her future life.

Later that spring, after the Beloit Class Day which
they had attended en masse, the sophomores atoned for
their sins by taking the juniors up the Rock River on

the little steamer *Transit* and allowing teachers and seniors to go along. The picnic baskets emptied of ham and buns, toasts began with the fruit. The sophomores rose with a swish of ruffles and lauded their rivals, while the seniors, waving bananas, also complimented the third-year girls on their charm and wisdom. Flushing to the high necks of their frocks, the juniors in a burst of inspiration compared the nine sophomores to the nine Muses.

Vacation seemed over the hills and far away, with final examinations and music recitals ahead. What if one should not pass? Jane's brother-in-law, the Rev. J. M. Linn, was one of the examining committee in Bible History and Mental and Moral Philosophy, but even a relative was little comfort when one stood all alone before these clergymen in chapel and answered questions. Afterwards, girls with damp ringlets pushed back from their flushed foreheads sat around the rooms on packed boxes and trunks, excitedly comparing notes:

"Was the committee very hard on you?"

"Were you much scared when you got up to read?"

Back for her last autumn at Rockford, Jane once more filed every morning into chapel with the other students, away for the moment from books and ink, and sat near the shuttered, high-arched windows to hear Miss Anna Sill read the brief service. Miss Sill, principal of this pioneer Seminary since the founding thirty years before, was a comely, forceful woman with young eyes. Her God was a righteous God, and she wanted her girls to serve Him as cultivated Christian women at home or, better, to carry His word abroad as missionaries. The girls loved her but were awed by her dignity. A true gentlewoman, she was proper in all things. When the new telephones came in, she could not bring herself to use a vulgar greeting like, "Hello," but said, "Who is it?"

The enthusiastic meetings of the Castalian and Vesperian literary societies were very different from the quiet morning worship in chapel. Once the Castalians decorated the chapel with statues and paintings, and proudly invited the townspeople out to hear the Italian Renaissance discussed. At another meeting Jane took the affirmative of the question:

"Resolved: the French women have had more influence through literature than politics."

Though Jane was agreed to be the school's best oratress, she had some faults of elocution, as her friends told her frankly. How could a young woman of twenty who girlishly let her voice fall at the end of sentences expect to win the Illinois Intercollegiate Oratorical Contest at Galesburg? So they groomed her in rolling phrases and dramatic gestures. She *must* win not only for Rockford but for Woman. Rockford was the first woman's school, and she was the first woman ever to be entered in this intercollegiate meet.

Arriving in Galesburg, Jane and her alternate were just in time to see the judges award the prizes. The contest was over—they had mistaken the date!

With a chuckle at this fiasco after all the fuss Rockford had made, Jane posed among the more punctual elocutionists for a cabinet photograph. She sat next to a gentleman with sideburns and across from a smooth-shaven youth who gazed admiringly at Woman. The six other speech-makers stood behind in a semicircle, wearing long frock coats, winged collars, and black

ties. With her close-fitting surah frock arranged to show
the bow on the overskirt and the pleats underneath,
Jane looked much too slim and dainty ever to have de-
fended Woman's cause against these towering, solemn
young men. The tallest of them all was William Jennings Bryan, who had his right arm thrust Napoleon-
ically inside his coat and had not a hair out of place on
his sleek black head. Even then young Bryan, future
leader of the Democratic party, was a silver-tongued
orator. He just had won the contest's second prize of
fifty dollars and already was planning to spend the
money on a garnet engagement ring for his sweetheart,
Mary Baird.

Next morning Jane persuaded her companion to go
with her down to Jacksonville to visit the state institu-
tions for the blind and for the deaf and dumb. The sight
of these handicapped children touched Jane deeply.
With little thought for oratorical contests, she returned
to Rockford only to find her schoolmates quite sharp
with anxiety about the outcome of the Galesburg affair.

On Election Day in November, the results of a straw
vote for President were read in the chapel, which had

been festively draped in the Stars and Stripes. The votes were ninety for James A. Garfield, ten for General Winfield Scott Hancock. Cheering lustily for Garfield, the Republicans rose and sang *The Star-spangled Banner,* and the Democrats for Hancock had to stand up too. As Rockford went, so went the Union, for Garfield was elected President by a high sheaf of votes. The stanch Seminary Republicans, among them Jane, had their reward in a feast on twelve fat turkeys from the farm of a generous Republican, and they gave the necks and gizzards to the Democrats.

The seventeen seniors were busy with their own election campaign and again chose Jane Addams president of their class of '81. Jane also was editor-in-chief of the Rockford *Seminary Magazine.* Her first issue printed school news; a poem, *Carissima;* and the articles *Beyond the Caucasus Lies Power, A Short Trip into Mongolia, The Last Great Empire, Surprise Party,* and *The Skeleton in My Closet.* Editorially, Jane wrote:

"Our editor's sanctum is to be, we hope, a success this year; a place to which we can withdraw to invite the few thoughts we possess to flow more freely; a place made attractive by every surrounding; in fact, a delightful little haven. The editor's easy chair has thus far been a dream. The scrap basket, to which so much really valuable material has been consigned for lack of room, takes its place in bold relief, and materials for writing stand so delightfully that to seize a pen and write will be the very essence of happiness. This cosy little retreat is hereafter to be kept sacred to the editors. A box for communications will be placed on or near the door, and we hope it will always be full. If every student will but feel a personal interest in the welfare of the Seminary Magazine and do all in her power to support it, it cannot but be a success."

Now the seniors had the dignity of holding conclaves in their own elegant parlors, with walls hung in rich dark paper sprinkled with wheat sheaves and floor laid with a Brussels carpet of gold and poppy red. No junior ever had the impudence to stick her nose inside these sacred precincts. Far from settling idly back on the parlor upholstery, the seniors planned a breakfast for the famous educator, venerable Mark Hopkins, of whom President Garfield had said, "A log with a student at one end and Mark Hopkins at the other is my ideal college."

That same year when an even more ancient celebrity, Amos Bronson Alcott, visited the Seminary, the freshmen were excited because he was the father of Louisa May Alcott and the seniors, because he was an intimate of their idolized Ralph Waldo Emerson. To do him humble service, Jane even cleaned the mud from the Alcott storm boots and was rewarded with the mild radiance of his smile.

As the days of her senior year grew into months, Jane was being pressed to join the Congregational or the Presbyterian church and go to Turkey as a missionary. The Seminary, chartered in 1847 as a "goodly plant" to "secure high intellectual culture and especially to develop moral and religious character," had sent many noble women to foreign fields. Jane, with her intelligence and gift for leadership, would make an ideal missionary, the faculty thought. But Jane did not feel the call either to join a church or to Christianize the heathen.

Though frequent prayers were said for the girls who remained outside the fold of the church, Jane stood her ground politely but steadfastly. She felt that church membership was not necessary in order to believe in

God and lead a good life—her father, a non-member, was as upright a man as one might find. Nor did being a foreign missionary appeal to her so much as studying medicine and serving the American poor. So the school found a will of iron in the gentle young woman. What she did not believe in, she did not believe. Always be honest with yourself, her father had taught her. A few years later she was to become a member of the Presbyterian church, but she did not feel ready to join now.

Jane lost no popularity by her stubborn courage, and the seniors unanimously elected her valedictorian, the highest honor in the Seminary. Her grades probably would have made her valedictorian anyway, but her friends asked to acclaim her themselves. Nora Frothingham was named salutatorian.

Since Jane was to give the valedictory address, she meant to speak clearly and directly. "Let's *say* something, Nora," she urged, impatient at thought of orations she had sat through, orations as long and pompous as they were empty.

And "say something" they did on Commencement Day. Nora's subject was *Monopolies*, and Jane talked of

Cassandra, fated Trojan prophetess whose tragedy it was "always to be in the right, always to be disbelieved and rejected." She compared with Cassandra's gift of prophecy the intuition of Woman which sees and feels lies and injustice but makes no attempt to prove them:

"There is a way opened, women of the nineteenth century, to convert this wasted force to the highest use. . . . only by the accurate study of at least one branch of physical science can the intuitive mind gain that life which the strong passion of science and study feeds and forms. . . . With eyes accustomed to the search for Truth, she [Woman] will . . . test whether her intuition is genuine and a part of nature, or merely a belief of her own. . . ."

Jane's flute-like voice proclaimed:

"Having gained accuracy. . . . In active labor she will be ready to accept the promptings that come from growing insight, and when her sympathies are so enlarged that she can weep as easily over a famine in India as a pale child at her door, then she can face social ills and social problems as tenderly and as intuitively as she can now care for and understand a crippled factory child. . . .

"The opening of the ages has long been waiting for this type of womanhood. . . . Now is the time for a faint realization of this type, with her faculties clear and acute, from the study of science, and with her hand upon the magnetic chain of humanity. . . ."

Turning, Jane addressed her classmates, "the glorious seventeen." "If you are tempted to flag and grow weary in 'bread-giving,' remember the sixteen girls of '81 who believe and expect high things of you.

"God be with you."

She finished in a silence so deep that the swallows could be heard twittering outside under the eaves, and then the chapel echoed applause. The slender girl of twenty stood there in simple white, as lovely as the first Cassandra, and then she walked away. Soon she was to be the woman the world would know "with her hand upon the magnetic chain of humanity."

"Write to me," cried each girl of "the glorious seventeen" with the parting kiss.

"Don't forget me."

"Good-by, good-by, good-by."

8

LIFE GOES ON

IN AUGUST Jane was on holiday, traveling with her family along the red ore roads of northern Michigan to visit the copper mines. The Seminary was behind, and all life ahead. Too happy even to think, she breathed the spicy air of the pine woods or leaned over the carriage side to buy raspberries from tow-headed little girls. Miners' shacks climbed up the sides of old diggings, and boats sailed in off cold blue Lake Superior with silver cargoes of fish. The brilliance of those August days and, above all, the delight of being with her father stayed in Jane's mind through all the years to come.

Without warning John Addams, always strong and well, felt sharp pains. They tried to get him home to

Cedarville, but, in a hotel at Green Bay, Wisconsin, he died. Always he had been near Jane for comfort and for counsel, to love and be loved, and now her adored father was gone. It was the greatest sorrow she had ever known or would know. Sitting in the hotel window and looking down at the street through her tears, she wondered how people could be buying groceries and playing phonographs—how life could be going on—with her father dead.

As the cold fall rains set in, Jane began to pack feverishly; the busier she was, the less time for brooding. Perhaps, studying at the Woman's Medical College in Philadelphia, she could forget a little; and later, as a doctor among the poor, she could realize some of the high ideals of public service which her father had cherished. Mrs. Addams and George, sister Alice and her husband Harry were going to Philadelphia as well. Soon the shutters of the Cedarville home were closed, the furniture covered, and the fires put out for the first time since the house had been built by the young John Addams in the first flush of his success in Illinois.

Though Jane found medicine quite interesting and

was able to pass examinations with success, she could not recover from the nervous shock of her father's sudden death. Bravely she tried to remember that all the races of men knew sorrow, but already the old pains were alive in her back. For tortured days and nights in the spring, she had to lie on a hospital bed in Philadelphia. After examining her gravely, a noted specialist called Harry Haldeman aside to say, "She'll not live a year."

"You don't know her. She'll outlive us all," replied Harry with spirit.

By early summer, Jane was strong enough to return to Rockford and receive her bachelor degree, her A.B., with Catherine Waugh and two others. Rockford Seminary was no more; it was Rockford College now, and one of the oldest women's colleges in the United States! The organ pealed triumph as the girl graduates marched down the aisle in their white dresses with perky sashes. Always before, the sashes had been tied in back, but the trustees had solemnly decided that the bow could now be moved more fashionably to the side. The home-like buildings, the worn steps, the laughing girls were the same as the year before, but Jane was not. She looked older, more frail, and, though she smiled as always, the sadness in her eyes made her friends want to cry.

Her back troubling her again, Jane went out to Mitchellville, Iowa, to stay with her capable sister Alice. Strapped to a bed, she lay patiently for six months after her twenty-second birthday, passing the time reading. Alice tried to make her forget her pain, while Harry used his best medical science to help her. Then she was put into a plaster cast for weeks before she could go to Chicago and have a leather jacket made. This steel-ribbed jacket fitted down to the hips and acted as a crutch under her arms to take the pressure off her spine. Though the stays and leather were heavy, she was relieved of incessant ache and felt so much better that she began planning a trip abroad.

There were to be eight in the traveling party—Mrs. Addams and a young kinswoman, Sarah Hostetter; the Penfields, a cheery old lady and her daughter; and Mary Ellwood, a wealthy Rockford classmate of Jane's, Mary's sister, and their aunt. They all shed good-by tears at their last glimpse of "big beautiful majestic Brooklyn Bridge"; but the salty breeze and August sun soon acted "like magic," and Jane was writing farewell letters to be dropped off at Sandy Hook.

Waves looked high as two-story houses to them as they steamed out into the open sea in the *Servia* of the Cunard Royal Line. That first day, everyone was giddy and seasick, but by next morning Mrs. Addams was vivaciously going around meeting people. Jane and Mary Ellwood, her cabin-mate, were not such good sailors, and for several days the kippered herring, the pasties, and the roast beef on the menu were hateful words. Fog followed the wind, and they needed their "nobby" ulsters, steamer rugs, and hot-water bags against the clammy mist.

"Is it always foggy?" they asked the deck steward.

"I don't live here," he answered in the tone reserved for passengers' foolish questions.

Finding her "sea-legs" at last, Jane walked the decks to get color in her sallow cheeks and cried out at night over the shining beauty of the phosphorescence flashing from the dark waves. Of the notables on the passenger list she wrote to Alice: "Theodore Thomas [the great Chicago orchestra leader] and some of his friends are on board. I saw him sitting today on the same bench with a small boy who was playing a jews-harp; he was watching him with a mixture of good natured contempt and kindly amusement which made his face very pleasant to remember. Celebrity No. two is Henry James, the novelist, who I look at most of the time between courses at table—he is very English in appearance, but not especially keen or intellectual."

As land neared, Mary burst into the stateroom with a purse of English crowns and shillings, exclaiming, "We must practice using this stuff or we will be cheated out of our very eyes."

Strangely quiet with the engines stopped, the *Servia* anchored off the rolling hills of Ireland, having made a quick crossing in a little over seven days. Screaming gulls flapped out to meet the steamship, and a tug took off mail, baggage, and passengers, among them the Addams party waving forlorn handkerchiefs at newly-made friends on board. Their six trunks past the Queenstown customs, they traveled second-class to Cork and from there drove out to ivy-covered Blarney Castle, followed by a saucy mob of children begging pennies from the "Yankees."

"We climbed up the powerful old tower but could not reach the Blarney stone with our lips," Jane wrote. "A young Englishman managed to kiss it and then offered to hand it around second hand but we refused."

Delighted with the folklore and castled beauty of the Killarney Lakes, they journeyed on to Dublin past thatched peasant cottages and the stone walls of country estates. Because a rainy day gave Mrs. Addams chills and fever, they stayed ten days in Dublin, nursing her and reading Irish history cozily before an open fire. Jane happened to mention England to a chatty old man whom she met on an omnibus, and was startled to have him flare, "They have gone too far-r, too far-r. We can't stand it any longer. . . . I'm going to speak my mind now if it ruins me."

The other passengers stirred uneasily, and Jane realized that she had met "the Irish question" face to face. Shortly, this young woman of twenty-three observed: "I have seen more cosey places and more wretched places in Ireland than ever before. The amount of dirty ragged children in the streets is appalling, but they are so impudent, jolly, and continually begging that it is hard to pity them. . . . We had a ride today through the crowded city and although the day was fine and sunny and some of the streets gay and animated one felt everywhere almost as a palpable pressure—the wretchedness and misrule, and that it is deeper than anything government can reach."

Seasickness on the *Servia* and rest in Ireland had done her good, Jane thought, and she felt almost well again. Her back had grown so much stronger that she was able to discard the ill-fitting jacket in "enchanting" Edinburgh and to travel long hours by coach reading history and poetry from the map of Scotland. Close by the field where Robert Burns plowed up the mouse, "wee, sleekit, cowrin', tim'rous beestie," Jane stooped to pick a purple flower.

"Stay yer hand, lass," cried the guide.

"And why?"

"Ye mus'na pick th' faery thimble, 'r th' faeries'll follow ye to nae guid."

9

HUNGRY HANDS

WITH Scottish harebells and ivy from Words-
worth's cottage pressed in books for remem-
brance, the Addams party arrived in London and went
straight to a boarding house kept by New England sisters. The foggy old city seemed to them appallingly
huge as they tried to "take in" all the miles of paintings
and museum cases and time-stained buildings. But of
Westminster Abbey Jane wrote rapturously:

"We had a bag full of books to do it up as best we
could, but some way there was nothing of that kind to
be done. It is like a production of pure thought or
creation of the mind alone, and you can't imagine men
ever *building* it."

A hilarious visit to Madame Tussaud's waxworks

lightened the heavy museum work for the eight Americans. They wandered giggling about the costumed figures of "famous and infamous persons," so real that Puss Ellwood tried to give her ticket to a doorman labeled "the late Charles Dickens." Mrs. Penfield stared long at a policeman before she asked him, "Are you wax too?"

He winked and replied, "I wish I was, leddy, so 'elp me. Maybe I wouldn't be so 'ot."

"This is the first real lark we've had," exulted Mary Ellwood.

Taking cabs and railway carriages by storm, the eight made a side trip to see the towers and domes of Oxford and go on to Shakespeare's own Stratford-on-Avon. Here ale was running so freely that the old caretaker wouldn't unlock Shakespeare's birthplace for fear of the servant rabble hiring out to new masters for the year.

Jane had peeped at "Vanity Fair" riding forth with powdered lackeys in Hyde Park, but she wanted as well a glimpse of the seamy side of London. Eagerly she took the opportunity to visit the "East End" with one of the

HUNGRY HANDS

New England sisters atop an omnibus on a Saturday midnight. Clattering along, close to second-story windows where tired clerks and dock hands, match girls and kitchen maids lay asleep and dreamed of Sunday pork and holiday clothes, and past brawling taverns, they lurched on into a street of market stalls.

Here torches flared cruelly on the grabbing hands, the hungry hands, the desperate hands of London's homeless and starving. Men in broken hats and soleless shoes fought women in torn shawls for places near the booths.

"Sixpence for th' sack o' potatoes?" roared a huckster. "Five pence? Four pence? Thruppence? Yer lyin', cheatin' blighter bids tuppence 'a'penny, an' I'm givin' hit to 'im."

Hands grabbed the sack and carried it away.

"Throw down yer dirty money, yer wharf rats."

Greedy hands reached out for rotting carrots and snatched at fish and turnips too spoiled to be saved for the Monday market. And in the shadows other wretches without money waited to search the gutters for crusts of bread and dig through garbage boxes for bones.

Never in all her sheltered life had Jane seen such misery. She shivered in her warm cloak and felt ashamed of her full purse. The torchlight burned the memory of these hungry hands into her mind. Wasn't there someone somewhere who could see that people got enough to eat, who could—right the wrongs of the world?

London did try to care for its deserted children Jane discovered that Sunday, when, sad and perplexed, she went to the old Foundling Hospital and watched the little girls, in 'kerchiefs and high white caps, and the little boys praying in chapel and eating dinner afterwards.

Over the Channel and past the windmills of Holland, the Americans hurried on to Germany. Mrs. Addams could speak the language fluently and Jane dived into her German dictionary. As they worried over the customs, Puss Ellwood exclaimed, "What fun it would be to travel if we didn't have any baggage!"

The Prussian cavalrymen, drilling before the palace of Sans Souci at Potsdam, were so handsome that Mary Ellwood couldn't stop admiring them, and she had to be fairly dragged into the palace. They were met by a funny, button-nosed guide who made them slip soft shoes over their sharp heels before allowing them to walk on polished floors kings had trod. With a worried look at their gliding feet, he warned, "Pe slow ven you skate."

Though royalty had left this wide-spreading palace for the winter, the travelers soon learned that they were to be on the Berlin train with two German princesses. Pressing noses against the glass of their railway carriage, the Americans saw gorgeous footmen standing at attention and policemen keeping the crowds back. Then the station door opened, and two modest little princesses dressed in black walked quickly down a red carpet, looking embarrassed at all the commotion.

"I felt like quoting Horace. 'The mountains labored and brought forth a mouse,' " Jane wrote in one of her chatty letters home.

When she heard the great Russian pianist Rubinstein in Berlin, Jane was restless at first, but in the end wished that he would never stop playing.

"He is very homely," she recorded frankly. "Has no

bridge at all to his nose—but looking at his head as a whole there is something very powerful in it—and a nervous tense organization is evident in every move he makes. . . . It was our first experience in taking off our hats and cloaks. I like the custom immensely, it is much easier to listen freed of a hat."

Settled in winter quarters at Dresden in a pension kept by a kindly old German couple, they hunted out a German teacher; and Puss Ellwood began to paint and Sarah Hostetter to sing. Though Jane's health was improving fast, she had few plans beyond studying German, catching up on history, mounting views in an album, and going to the opera and to the art gallery with its famous *Sistine Madonna* by Raphael.

"The Sistine Madonna is in a room alone," she informed her sister Mary. "Men take off their hats and stand as if in a church. You feel when you look on the divine faces as if you would never do a mean thing again; of course you come down and probably do something trifling on the way home—but it never fails to make the same impression."

Christmas close and America so far away made them

all blue and homesick. Wandering through the market stalls with their gilt balls and wax angels, gingerbread men and toy villages, Jane longed for her small nephews and niece, and wistfully wrote for news of "everything" about Christmas at home. But, after a real German Christmas dinner and a frolic, not even the girl who had been given a big red handkerchief felt moved to cry in it.

In her travels, Jane was seeing much that she wanted to remember always and was busy matching historic people to places, but occasionally she was as gorged on beauty and as tired of sight-seeing as Sarah who exclaimed, "I hope I never see another picture as long as I live!"

Everywhere Jane had met other well-chaperoned American girls studying music and languages, and making daily trips to art galleries and museums, seeking culture as she was. Sometimes all this seemed so selfish, when the poor were suffering, that she revolted from mere culture.

One January morning in Coburg, after they had left Dresden and were moving southward toward Italy, she climbed from her feather bed and dressed near the white porcelain stove. Blowing a hole in the frost on the inn window, she looked out over the snowy market square. There she saw a dozen peasant women carrying on their backs heavy casks so full of hot beer that it splashed in scalding drops upon their heads and shoulders. Hardly waiting to button her jacket, Jane ran across the square to protest to the brewery owner.

"Look at those women," she cried. "Couldn't the beer be carried in some other way?"

"Ach Himmel, und who says it should pe?" he blustered, very red in the face.

"I do," replied Jane, suddenly feeling very small indeed and going back to the inn with no taste for breakfast coffee and rolls.

Her heart ached when she discovered that the women worked thus from five in the morning until seven at night for a pitiful thirty-eight cents a day. Sights of other women drudging along under manure baskets and of smoke pouring out of dreary, chimneyless hovels made her even more miserable, and she was glad to leave southern Germany for Trieste and a boat to Venice.

HUNGRY HANDS

In the gray February afternoon, the Grand Canal showed such decaying glory that they all agreed at first with Puss Ellwood's remark:

"I should think there would be lots of suicides here—the water is so convenient."

Country women stopped rubbing clothes on the rocks of a muddy creek to watch three foreign young ladies walking along the road to Rome in the blazing March sun. The dark cypresses, narrow as exclamation points, gave no shade, and ox-carts whirled dust on the walkers, on the silver-green olive trees, and on the musk-fragrant yellow balls of the mimosa. Jane, Mary, and Sarah, with heads steaming and petticoats held high, were marching on Rome over the old Flaminian Way, as pilgrims had done for hundreds of years. Having arrived in Rome the night before by train, they had hurried after breakfast to hire a rickety old man in a rickety old victoria to drive them three miles out from the city walls and leave them just where the great dome of St. Peter's first snowed above the blue line of the sky, just where pilgrims to the Eternal City cried, "Ecce Roma!"

Through the Porta del Popolo near a stone worn by pilgrim knees, the American girls passed with peasant women balancing wine jugs on their heads and with goats led in to be milked from door to door. And on went the three weary pilgrims under clusters of purple bougainvillea hanging from every lattice, feeling already that it was "like undertaking to see the world itself to see all of Rome's sights."

After a month in Rome, Jane, Sarah, and Mrs. Addams bade farewell to the Ellwoods and crossed Italy's boot to take a steamer for Greece. Jane sighed that she would prefer a visit in Cedarville just now to one in Athens; but her zest for travel soon returned, and she was writing from Athens:

"We had honey for breakfast from Mt. Hymettus, it was delicious and quite up to our idea of Ambrosia. . . . The striking costumes in the streets [of the baggy-trousered Turks] make us almost feel as if we were in an oriental country. The hotel is very comfortable. All the waiters look like heathen and speak very good English. . . . The views of the Acropolis with the ruined temples is very fine from our window. (And if we were not so thoroughly shaken by the sea we would no doubt have rushed to it the first thing.) . . . The sky is very soft, but the rim is white and glaring and no foreigner pretends to go out in the middle of the day without an umbrella and blue glasses. . . . We most sincerely hope the Mediterranean will be lenient to us [en route to Naples]. I never saw such blue water, it is just exactly the shade of a tub of 'blueing' to rinse clothes in. . . ."

Unfortunately, Old Aeolus unbagged all his winds on the cruise to Naples, and Jane was so ill for a day that she couldn't move from the sofa in the ladies' cabin. The steward came in with a fresh-laid egg, and later Jane wrote, "Just at that moment an egg was the most repulsive thing on earth and an egg laid by a seasick hen was unendurable."

On her feet once more, Jane peered into the belching crater of Vesuvius and laughed at the Capri donkey woman who tried to wheedle an extra tip from Sarah by telling her that she was astride "an American jackass." But again, Jane saw wretchedness—the blind Neapolitan beggars and the naked children sitting in gutters eating macaroni. Just ahead of the dread cholera, they left Italy, and in Paris Jane and Sarah splurged on a "toney" traveling dress apiece. Jane's was so tight that she had to take it off and put on her ulster in order to write, and Sarah blurted, "The idea of two country girls coming to Paris and getting dresses that they are only comfortable in when they sit perfectly quiet!"

They showed more strength of mind in the jewelry shops of the Palais Royal: "This is the place in which American women always ruin their finances, and we wondered when we went in whether it were possible for four women to come out without buying anything. We inspected everything—absolutely hurt one's eyes from the dazzle of the diamonds—and came out unscathed."

George Haldeman, who was abroad for the summer, was awaiting them in Switzerland, and they joined him there for new adventures. Up a steep desolate mountain they rode on horseback through an Alpine thunderstorm, and reached one of the highest hotels in Europe just as a rainbow banded the Rhone Valley far below. Jane and Sarah doffed their streaming clothes and went to bed at once, eating supper off a pillow propped up between them.

After a hasty morning look at the ice-grottoes of the magnificent Rhone Glacier, they started back down at seven, only to flee from more rain into a quaint old chalet and finally to descend in a whirling snowstorm to the sunlit valley.

"If you can stand all that, you are good for anything," declared Sarah, and Jane agreed between sniffles.

When George left for America, he carried away a box for the rest of the family, and the news that Jane was almost as strong as ever. She had gained seventeen pounds and now weighed a bouncing hundred and fifteen. The box held gifts and purchases made by Jane on order—a cane from Waterloo battlefield, leather slippers from Athens, bear chessmen and a cuckoo clock from Switzerland, corals and cameos, mosaics and laces.

With George gone and Sarah too, Jane and Mrs. Addams looked yearningly at the family photographs arranged about their Berlin sitting room, but held firm to their resolve of staying abroad another year to study more and travel less.

The other American guests in the pension envied their cozy quarters and often tapped on the door with a forlorn, "May I come in and sit by your stove for half an hour? I am positively frozen. This is the only comfortable room I've seen since I have been in Europe."

Jane informed Alice cheerily, "The German and French lessons go along smoothly and between reading up for my lecture and writing the notes out in German afterwards I seem to be about as busy as I was at school; with this difference, that there is no necessity about it and the gay operas and changes come in between very often."

When she asked at the American Exchange for news of the Presidential election in the United States, a young clerk informed her that Grover Cleveland had won for the Democrats so far, but that the final results were not yet known. Like a true Republican, Jane "still allowed myself to hope."

African-tanned Henry Stanley, the Congo explorer, was the lion of the brilliant Thanksgiving dinner for Americans at the Englishes Haus. "It was a full dress white kid occasion . . . but we are glad to believe it our last Thanksgiving this side of the Atlantic," Jane wrote.

Driving out from Berlin in a crowded carriage, the American girl saw the huntsmen and hounds of young Prince William's first wild boar chase. Indeed, she saw everything save the boar himself, including hard-riding Prince William whose left arm was shriveled. Perhaps she remembered this view of him when, in 1914 as Kaiser William II, he led his nation into the World War.

Glamorous views of Sarah Bernhardt, playing to a packed theater in Paris, and of fiery old Victor Hugo, receiving admirers in his home, were also left to Jane before she at last sailed homeward.

10

HOME AGAIN AND AWAY

A CUPOLA torn off, porches built on, a few more
stones in the cemetery, new babies, fresh stocks
of calico at the general stores, hollyhocks in the door-
yards—Cedarville had not changed much when Jane
came back after two years abroad. The summers were
delightful here among the cool rustlings of the trees in
a countryside washed by rain and dried by sun.

Two winters Jane spent in Baltimore with her stepmother and George, who was studying science at Johns
Hopkins University and making such beautifully exact
drawings of a rare creature from the sands of North
Carolina that these later were sent to the British Museum. Though Jane took lecture courses, she did not
go back to the medical student's grind, for she had long

since given up her plan to be a doctor among the poor, feeling that was not her calling.

Growing deep within her, however, was a burning desire to be of service to humanity and a sharp distaste for the idle life of travel and study, alternating with invalidism, which she had been leading since her graduation from Rockford. Surely at twenty-seven she had done little to fulfill the clarion call of Commencement Day, "Remember the girls of '81 who believe and expect high things of you."

Was she to lose herself in vague dreams and do nothing to make her life worth having lived it? As yet she had had only glimpses of the suffering in the world, but these were enough to make her ashamed of her own ease and comfort. She felt herself to be a pale shadow living on books, while outside in the world men were struggling for jobs and women were going without food that their children might eat. She was standing aside doing nothing—nothing! Scornfully she applied to herself the words of a German poet:

"I use my love of others for a gilding to make myself
more fair."

Seeking she knew not exactly what, Jane restlessly wandered back to Europe with friends. In Paris, she discovered that she had forgotten so much French that she got mutton chops when she thought she ordered veal. Her first trip had been well-chaperoned, but this time she was quite independent, mistress of a fair fortune of sixty-five thousand dollars which her father had left her out of his quarter-million estate.

"I am quite impressed with the difference in my age and dignity between this trip to Europe and the one before," she informed Alice from Germany. "*Then* I was Mademoiselle and Fräulein and I felt like a young girl. I went to this hotel alone and ordered a room for the night, and was obliged to spend a night alone at the hotel in Munich. Everywhere it was 'Madame' with the utmost respect and I felt perfectly at my ease and dignified all the time."

It was to be a more thoughtful, philosophic journey. "Have lost that morbid thirst for information and doing that simply consumes American travelers and certainly did me the last time."

Meeting Ellen Starr, on holiday from her art classes at

an exclusive girls' school in Chicago, Jane settled with
her in Munich to study Italian. Her enthusiasm for this
Rockford friend was at a peak, not because of "her
cleverness which is a constant source of pleasure to me,
but for her persistent effort to get the *best* in the world,
the highest and truest, and her efforts for *patience* to
work it out in her own character."

The two were a mutual admiration society in themselves, for Ellen declared of her dear "Jeannie":

"I wish I could paint her or write her or put her into
music to do the whole world good, as she does me; but
I can only keep her in my heart to try to be just a little
like her, with very limited success. Yesterday I lost my
temper. I have lost it frequently before but it seemed
wickeder to me to lose it after being for two months
so near her. . . . I think she would be horribly shocked
if she could see what I have written. She seems to shrink
so from anything of that sort that I ever say in praise of
her. . . ."

Ellen was quivering with ecstasy over the art of
Europe. In her raptures about Dürer, she nearly froze
her feet wading through the snowdrifts to his tomb.

Somewhat ruefully she exclaimed afterwards, "Well, I am glad that I brushed the snow off of Albrecht Dürer's inscription if it did ruin my last gloves."

Even with her black broadcloth traveling suit and her fur cloak, Jane found the weather bitter; but, ignoring their chilblains, they continued on into Italy, for, as Ellen tartly remarked, "We didn't have presence of mind enough to change our plans when the weather turned from Italian into Greenlandic."

But Rome was warm under a flashing sky when Jane set forth to study the Catacombs, those burrows dug for miles underground by the early Christians. Here they had fled from the Romans to escape being torn by hungry lions in the Colosseum, here they had buried their dead, and here sung the glory of Christ.

Jane's Catacomb explorations ended abruptly with a bad attack of sciatic rheumatism which put her under an American nurse's care for weeks. Though sometimes her leg was knotted with pain, Jane was more troubled about upsetting the plans of Ellen and of another friend and insisted that they go on to southern Italy without her.

Lying there in bed, her rheumatic leg stretched out stiffly, Jane was at the mercy of her two selves which now began to talk. How useless you are, accused the first self, and what a pretender! But, said the second self, I'm trying to understand the artists' sympathies for mankind when I visit galleries and cathedrals, and in the Catacombs I want to feel the all-embracing love of the early Christians. Really now, retorted the first self, are you being honest? Isn't it true that you just like to look at pictures and just like to travel and take endless notes? You're going on and on. Have you forgotten the hungry hands of London and the beer carriers of Coburg? Have you forgotten the beggars of Naples and Ireland?

For several years now through the clouds that troubled her mind, Jane had had glimpses of the blue sky. She had a plan, invigorating in its simplicity, which she would carry through if she could but rouse herself from her musings. She would rent a house in some shabby district and be a neighbor to the poor, go hand in hand with the workers, trade her culture for a knowledge of humanity. Perhaps other young women also would leave the stuffy libraries with her and walk into the freshness of the streets. Long ago, as a girl of six, she had cried, "When I'm a grown-up lady, I want to live right next door to poor people, and the children can play in my yard."

Of course Jane's house would be in the United States and not in Europe. She was an American as all her hard-working, hard-thinking people had been for generations —farmers, millers, bankers, soldiers, legislators of the New World.

Afraid that talking might make the blue sky of the plan vanish again into cloud, she did not speak of it, even when Ellen Starr came back from Naples, "consumed with fleas," but sparkling over a visit to a monastery. To the surprise of Jane's English doctor, who was shocked that so delicate a person—"an invalid one might say"—was traveling in Europe without a member of her family, Jane improved steadily and wrote to Alice:

"He hasn't the remotest idea of the toughness of my constitution. . . . I do hope the [Alice's] rheumatism is better. When we are old we will sit together on the two corners of the fireplace and nurse our precious legs. Won't we? Bless you."

On Good Friday in Florence, Jane saw hundreds kneeling in the darkened churches, and on Easter Sunday passed within six feet of Queen Victoria's carriage. "She is neither beautiful nor graceful but *not* as red and homely as she is painted."

Rheumatic twinges sent Jane hurrying with a family friend over to the balmy French Riviera, where perfumers were harvesting violets, and roses hedged orange groves along the aquamarine sea. At breakfast she had preserved rose petals, and before dinner a view of "depraved Vanity Fair" gambling at Monte Carlo.

"I became quite interested in watching a fine looking Englishman who looked like a clergyman and was losing frightfully, and in a very pretty young girl who was dressed in full dinner costume; she wore fine fawn-colored gloves and merely pushed the gold back and forth with the tips of her fingers as if utterly indifferent to it. She had a great pile of it in front of her and was said to have been winning all afternoon."

Before a winter blast sweeping down from the Alps, Jane fled out of Marseilles, her fur coat closely buttoned and her sciatic leg on a hot-water bottle, only to be told by Americans just coming out of Spain that it was "all awful"; if you went by train, you wished you had gone by boat, and vice versa. But Jane was used to such tourist tales by now and continued on by train quite comfortably to Madrid, where with Ellen Starr she met most of the English colony.

On Sunday afternoon, they drove out to the Place of Bulls amid a throng of café loungers, mustachioed army officers, and black-eyed beauties with mantillas draped from their high combs. The orange sand of the arena and the snow-topped mountains beyond, against the blue Spanish sky, were dazzling in the white sunshine. To the blast of trumpets, a bull rushed out like a cannon ball and gored a horse whose rider plunged headlong.

"Brave bull," cheered the crowd, "more horses," and went on peeling oranges.

"Time for the death, matador," the onlookers shouted.

A matador strode proudly to the middle of the ring, his pigtail standing out stiffly and the sun glittering on the golden embroidery of his jacket and tight breeches. With a scarlet cape, he baited the furious bull until swiftly he went in over the horn and stabbed the on-rushing beast in the spine.

"Bravo, bravo," roared the crowd as the bull staggered and fell.

"Jeannie," whispered Ellen with white lips, "I can't stand this. Let's go."

"Wait for me outside with the others," said Jane. "I want to stay." And she sat while four bulls and a pitiful heap of horses were killed.

"Jane, you're as inhuman as the Spaniards. You liked it," scolded Ellen.

"Well, it was interesting," Jane admitted honestly.

To her, the barbaric splendor of the bull fight had suggested a Roman wild beast show or a tournament of knights. She stopped herself abruptly. What an attitude —to be able to watch cruelty and bloodshed because they had historic meaning! So this was the result of all the study and travel—no preparation for service but a dulling of human sympathy! She *must* leave her idle dreams and begin at once to act upon her house among the poor, or at least start talking about it. She would tell Ellen first of all.

"Why, Jeannie, how splendid! I'll live with you. We'll do it together." Ellen half-laughed, half-cried in her enthusiasm. "Foolish? Too idealistic? No. It's splendid!"

Old Madrid was a strange place for two American girls to be planning a social experiment that was to be world-famous; and yet, with its palaces and poverty, its beggars asleep in the sun, Madrid was not so strange. Every day, as the friends journeyed onward, their scheme became more real; it began to live in their minds. Writing nothing of all this to her sisters, Jane continued to regale them with travel adventures. Their crossing to Africa was another saga of seasickness, but, when the ship anchored off Tangier, Jane remembered:

"I went over the edge of the ship [into a small boat] hearing the captain saying something in a loud and reassuring voice about 'jeter dans l'embrace de Moor' and thinking that Shakespeare in French was not improved when a huge Othello seized me and laid me on top of Miss Anderson. Ellen came down very much better and adjusted all our heads. . . . We were all drenched by the waves but so grateful for water on our faces that we did not much care."

On an afternoon among the nightingales and rose thickets of Granada, Jane showed Ellen a magazine clipping she had saved for its account of London's Toynbee Hall, the first social settlement in the world. Here Jane would go for ideas on her own project, while Ellen went to Italy as chaperon for two schoolgirls. Back in America then, they would begin a search for their home among the poor.

Toynbee Hall had been established a few years before as a memorial to Arnold Toynbee, the Oxford tutor who had died at thirty-one, worn out by his work for social reforms. Here came the little milliners, the furniture polishers and clerks, and the silk weavers of East London. Young University men lived at the Hall and taught them French or carpentry, music or shorthand, boxing and English literature. There were a library, an athletic field, and a hall for parties. Toilers and scholars mixed, learning from each other.

With a Freeport friend who had just come to Europe, Jane attended meetings of the London match girls, who

were striking that summer of 1888, and heard the bold-
est of them talk.

"Can a girl keep herself decent on two dollars a
week?"

"Ain't yer sick o' livin' on bread an' lard an' tea?
Meat?—I just longs fer hit."

"An' 'ere's what's li'ble to 'appen to yer. I means
'phossy jaw.'" A pathetic girl with teeth and jaw-bone
eaten by phosphorus fumes was pushed onto the platform.

Sweeping Jane and her companion with them, the
girls thronged out of the labor hall, flirting their tawdry
plush hats at young men on street corners.

11

HULL-HOUSE

WHEN Mrs. O'Leary's cow kicked over the lamp and started the Great Chicago Fire, in October 1871, the square red-brick house a few blocks away near the corner of Halsted and Polk Streets did not burn. Perhaps the cow's act was legend, but the terrific fire was not, nor was the old house. A proud mansion of early Chicago when Charles Hull built it in 1856, it since had been a secondhand store and an old folks' home. Now, in 1889, a school furniture factory used the first floor for storage, and the second floor was let to lodgers who thought the attic was haunted. On one side of the house was a combined livery stable and undertaking parlor run by "the biggest little Irishman on the West Side," and on the other flank was a popular

Irish saloon, followed down the block by a German bakery and a Jewish junk shop.

The neighborhood had indeed changed as much as the dilapidated old mansion. Where once hoop-skirted ladies had crossed broad lawns to spring houses and arbors, now ragged children swarmed out of tenements and workers stitched in sweat shops. Driving by in a carriage, Jane Addams saw the house still with its gracious air, like a faded gentleman of the old school. Next day, she came back to look closer but could not find it. Yet here was where she wanted to live, on Chicago's West Side among the colorful patchwork of races—Italians, Russian and Polish Jews, Bohemians and Irish, Scandinavians and Rumanians, Germans, Swiss, French, and French Canadians. She wanted especially to settle near the Italians, for in her travels she had come to love their gay spirits and warm hearts.

This spring of 1889, Jane Addams was combing Chicago for her house among the poor. Chicago seemed the place to look; it had large Italian colonies, and, though bluff and grasping, it still remembered the easy democracy of the prairies.

A go-ahead, dollar-chasing metropolis was the Chicago of the late eighties, second city in the land and bragging that it would soon be larger than New York. Proudly Chicagoans sniffed the belching smoke of factories and trains, and pointed out the "skyscrapers" of twelve and thirteen stories towering downtown above the furbelows of post-Fire structures. Pedestrians cheerfully dodged horse- and cable-cars, hansom cabs, and delivery wagons, calling such traffic jams signs of progress. Under the fantastic clock-tower of the Board of Trade, grain kings made fortunes; or they retired among the marble busts and oil paintings of their mansions to figure losses. On Sundays, the "first families" rode through the parks behind footmen sitting high on the boxes of carriages shiny as patent-leather. But, like the bacon from the world-famed Union Stockyards, Chicago had between its fat, long strips of lean, the teeming back streets where Jane Addams proposed to live.

Though she knew few people in the city beyond her father's friends—Roswell B. Mason, Chicago Fire mayor, and Lyman Trumbull, whom Lincoln had helped to the United States Senate—Ellen Starr was well-acquainted, especially with the wealthy parents of her students at the Kirkland school on the North Side. These influential and fashionable people were impressed with Jane's sincerity when she talked to them of her plan; here was no wild-eyed reformer, they saw, but a cultured, earnest young woman. Newspaper articles also approved Miss Addams, cramming notices of her beside long columns boosting the World's Fair for Chicago.

Still, some of Jane's closest friends were horrified at the idea of her going down to live "among the anarchists," as folk suspiciously called most of the poor and foreign since the "murderous and dastardly bomb-throwing" at the Haymarket riot three years before. Kindness to the poor was not new, nor was charity, but the idea of being a neighbor to "such people" was. Even Mrs. Addams and George, who was now at home with a nervous breakdown (he was never to realize his promise as a scientist), thought the adventure an idealist's dream.

"You think I'm going to try to scoop up the ocean with a teaspoon, don't you?" Jane asked one skeptic.

Though truly doubting her health and strength, Jane resolutely continued with Ellen to search the shabby districts, guided by newspaper reporters and city missionaries. One night they burst into their boarding house on Delaware Place crying, "We've found it! We've found the house."

Color flushed Jane's pale cheeks and her gray eyes were black with rare excitement as she told the news to the teachers and art students around the supper table. There she stood in her green silk dress with a gold panel down the side Turkish fashion, talking fast.

"An old house on the corner of Halsted and Polk. Rent part of it. All run-down. We can repair it. Furnish it like a house anywhere else in town."

With the whole second floor and part of the first floor of the house rented for thirty dollars a month, Jane and Ellen called in men to plaster high cracking ceilings, patch roof leaks, polish the oak floors, and repair the only bathroom for blocks around. And they helped to scrape ugly paint off the mellow white marble fireplaces and off the rope-like carving around the tall doors and windows. On the walls, tinted ivory and gold, they hung a sculptured frieze of della Robbia's lyric *Singing Boys,* foreign etchings, star-eyed madonnas, and more treasures picked up abroad which would be "helpful to the life of mind and soul." The old house was like an old copper teakettle; the more they rubbed it, the more it glowed.

They furnished it in its own period with horsehair sofas, mahogany chairs, and walnut beds and bookcases; a piano and Oriental rugs also came out of two thousand dollars saved from Jane's income, and out of Ellen's slender purse. Placing an Italian jug on a mantel just where the morning sun patterned it, they stood off to admire, ecstatic as brides arranging a home.

"Aren't you afraid the poor people will steal some of these beautiful things or break them?" an astonished friend exclaimed.

"Why, no. Why should they?" Jane went on hanging starched white curtains.

The night of September 14, 1889, was the first they spent in the house. There were three of them that night —Jane, just twenty-nine, Ellen, slightly older, and motherly Miss Mary Keyser, who came to do the housework and ended by caring for half the neighbor children. Jane felt unreal and like two persons, one moving into the dreamed-of house, the other watching her. That first night they dropped into bed so tired that they carelessly left a door wide open, but no one of the fifty thousand people in this Nineteenth Ward robbed them, though the area was known as one of the "toughest" in the city.

The neighbors were suspicious of the strange doings in "t'ole Hull house." Why should a couple of "swells" come to live down here? They must have something to sell, or maybe they'd get you to change your church. Or perhaps they were sent by the government to spy on workmen and the unions. Maybe they were just "slumming" to see how poor folk live; none of their pity, thank you. Maliciously, the neighbor boys threw garbage on the porch and stones through the windows.

Going out to market, Miss Keyser invited the wives of the butcher, the baker, and the saloon keeper for tea, and they came, first out of curiosity and again out of liking. Then the girls from the school furniture factory were supper guests and said they'd be in a class reading

George Eliot. So people began to trickle in and tell around that the young ladies treated them fine. Miss Addams and Miss Starr didn't seem to want anything out of you but just to be sociable and give you a good time and perhaps teach you something. They could talk your own language too—Italian or German or French.

The poor folk, used to being cheated and lied to, found it hard to understand that they now had two American friends. And the parish priests, sure that this was a mission to get converts to another faith, warned their flocks to stay away.

Still, tired mothers heard about the house and left their babies when they went out to work, and black-eyed girls with gold hoops in their ears shyly asked to play the "pianna" for dancing. It was so pretty here with fires blazing on the hearths, and the two young ladies were so "nice" and didn't act "toney." Once accepted by the neighborhood, Jane Addams and Ellen Starr were soon waist deep in its stream of life and death, dressing new babies, closing the eyes of the dead. One stormy night, Jane went forth through unlighted streets to the bedside of a dying Italian boy who was calling for "da 'Mericana lady," to say good-by.

When crippled Katie died, her mother sobbed to Jane Addams, "If I'd only o' known Katie was dyin', I'd've sat by her that las' day. But they told me she'd get better, an' I went out to work."

On New Year's Day, the old folk were invited to the house for an Old Settlers' Party. One wrinkled Irishman, still living in his old farmhouse, told how he had shot quail and prairie chickens round about in early days, and another said he had killed a deer just about where the house now stood.

"The 'furriners' are no good," these sages agreed darkly, "even if Miss Addams does like 'em."

Because the house was flanked by the undertaking parlor and the saloon, a humorist called the three, "Knight, Death, and the Devil." But the neighbors had their own name, "t'ole Hull house." So Hull-House became the name of what was to be the most famous social settlement in the United States. Only one American settlement had been started before it, although others quickly followed, and all were pioneers, blazing a trail through the wilderness of human needs and greeds.

"Hull-House was simply begun by two of us going down into the district to live. We had no definite idea as to what we were to do, but we hoped, by living among the people, to learn what was needed there and to help out," explained Jane Addams a few years later.

If the neighbors were curious about Hull-House, outsiders were more so; and visitors thronged in, hurrying their small boys in curls and velvet Lord Fauntleroy suits past jeering crowds hanging on the picket fence. Volunteers eagerly offered to help with clubs and classes. Some were society girls, and others were business men and women who boarded a dilapidated street car downtown and were pulled by a bony nag to Hull-House.

Now the place hummed with life, and it wasn't a question of whether neighbors would come but where they'd be put when they did. Before Jane and Ellen were through breakfast, a tousled tot would ring the bell, early for kindergarten, to tell them some breathless news like, "Pa came home awful drunk las' night," and to raid the table of oranges. Jumping on the furniture, splashing water in the bathtub, playing jungle under the palms, the kindergarteners made themselves at home; it was a neighborhood marvel that Hull-House could put up with them.

All morning these youngsters strung beads and played games in the drawing room with their guardian angel, pretty Miss Jennie Dow, a young Northsider. At noon they drank their milk and ate spaghetti, just throwing back their heads and opening mouths wide for great gobs. They liked dinner best of all, and pouted on Saturdays and Sundays because then they couldn't come.

Afternoons, the boys clamored around Miss Dow for stories of knights and kings and wars so stirring that they left checkers and jackstraws to hear and say, "Chees, dose guys had 's much guts 's cops."

They haunted museums on Saturdays, looking for such armor as brave Count Roland wore, fighting for Charlemagne. One day a boy close to tears almost ran into Miss Addams as he flounced out of the house, muttering, "I ain't comin' here no more. 'Sno use. Roland's dead."

Young Jews and Irish, smart as whips, took up all the chairs in library and dining room for evening College Extension classes. And workmen "let off steam" in the Social Science club by talking heatedly about what was wrong with government and jobs, and never by any chance agreeing with the business and civic leaders who addressed them. Warned by the Haymarket riot, Chicago felt the need of such a safety valve. The fact that Socialists, "single-taxers," and other radicals met in this club did not mean that Hull-House shared their views any more than it backed the Republicans and Democrats who also disputed.

On Friday nights, the Germans came—"men, women, and children taken in families as the Lord mixed them" —and sang the songs of the fatherland, a Grossmütter keeping time with her knitting needles. Or the young folk cheered their ruddy mother when she recited some poem by Goethe. They only had seen her cooking and washing and didn't know her mind held such a treasure.

In true Neapolitan fashion, Italian wives at first stayed home and sent their husbands to Hull-House parties, but gradually they too were drawn from their kitchens to dance the tarantella. By such friendly hospitality, Hull-House eased the fierce loneliness of a great city where families might live among thousands and yet be quite alone.

"Doc, why don't I grow?" an undersized boy of eight whispered to a doctor who brought the new baby.

But Hull-House itself had no need to ask such a question. Within this first year, it outgrew its original quarters and spread through the whole house, now given it rent-free by the generous owner. Though Jane Addams and Ellen Starr had started the settlement with their own money, they had, since the early months, been glad of the assistance of "The Tens." Twelve friends each persuaded ten people to give ten dollars for one month, making a hundred dollars monthly.

Jane—knowing well the value of money and carefully keeping books—found that they had spent over two thousand dollars that first year. A furnace had to be installed, for the house was too chilly with merely open fires for heat. Then the lawn had to be seeded and castor beans planted around the doorstep as a green oasis in this gray district. There was always something—

porches to be painted or broken windows replaced; and the neighborhood needed so much—rent and coal and groceries, medicine and baby clothes. Public baths were opened also, that men and women might wash off the sweat of labor.

To make their funds go farther, Jane and Ellen performed much of the janitor service, washing windows and mopping floors. They added weariness to weariness and could not stop. Only two years before in Rome, Jane had been a musing invalid, and now she was working too many hours to count, joyous in her usefulness. Something of the same fervor of creation with which artists paint masterpieces and authors write great novels carried her on through pain and fatigue.

Of the two young women, a journal wrote in this first year:

"To them it means something to forego the fascinations of fashionable society life, for which they are remarkably well adapted. The moving spirit in this novel philanthropy is Miss Addams. . . . She is a young lady, still quite young enough to make her choice of such a life-work, with all the sacrifices it involves, a seven-

days' wonder to all who know her. . . . Miss Addams'
rarest attraction—although possessing her share of physical beauty—is her wonderful spirituality. . . .

"Miss Starr supplements Miss Addams completely.
She is full of vivacity, a rare conversationalist, and one
who never loses sight of the humorous side of things.
She is a great favorite in society, with young and old,
men and women. Petite, graceful, brilliant, even to
sparkling, she adds to the combination what could by
no means be left out. . . ."

When a baby died across the street and Miss Starr
hung Fra Angelico's divine angel faces above the tiny
coffin, the other children said those angels robed in blue
and gold had taken away their sister. It comforted them
to think so. Many families asked to take various prints
of famous paintings home for a while, and a loan collec-
tion of pictures was started. One tired young factory
girl hung them all around her wretched little room.

"I lie on my bed just looking at the pretty things," she
explained. "It's so like art class."

Small rough Giuseppi, thumbing through the prints
to find one for his grandmother, held up a madonna,
"Dere's Jesus an' His mother."

"Yes, you can tell it by a certain celestial . . ." began the art teacher eagerly.

"No, it ain't dat. I tells 'em by da hoops on da back of da heads."

A widow, who went out to work each day, had to lock her children in the tenement flat with porridge on the table for lunch and a bed to crawl into if they got cold. They pounded on the door, crying, "Let us out, let us out," until Jane Addams heard about them. Already she knew of babies crippled for life by being tied too long to table legs or by falling out windows when mothers were away. In summer, mites shut out of the hot rooms toddled into Hull-House, clutching pennies in their moist little hands and offering them for the glasses of milk and thick slices of bread-and-butter. So badly was a day nursery needed for such forlorn youngsters that Jane Addams finally told one of her wealthy friends. Generously, the woman offered to finance a crèche, the tender French word for "crib," in a low cottage near Hull-House.

Here the working mothers—and fathers too—now brought their babies in the early mornings, washed and unwashed, fed and unfed, crying or still asleep in their blue blankets. Five cents a day the mother paid if she could, nothing if she couldn't. The white cribs and doll-size tables and chairs were there for them all—Italian bambinos and German kinder, sturdy Bohemians, and red-headed Irish. They sucked thumbs and spilled milk on bibs with right good will, prattling to the infant Jesus in pictures on the walls and sometimes giving Him juicy kisses.

Jane Addams of Hull-House was becoming a vogue in Chicago. Clubs asked her to talk, and she did with directness, without oratory, her hands clasped behind, her head thrown back, using ideas instead of gestures, never failing to "say something."

"The division of the city into rich and poor, into clean and unclean streets, is beginning to make us all uncomfortable"; or, "The rich need the poor as much as the poor need the rich."

Perhaps she would add, ". . . we might as well expect the granite Tower of the great Chicago Auditorium to float in mid-air without the substructure to uphold it and give it reason for being, as to hope for any uplift in our civilization without the underpinning and support of the masses. . . ."

Audiences, looking at her graceful profile and soft masses of brown hair, were startled. They had expected to see some battle-scarred crusader, and here was a gentle young woman, slender as a girl, with wonderfully expressive eyes and a magnetic personality.

"Oh, Jane, Jane, how do you do it?" exclaimed a friend. "If we only had your simplicity, we might do something."

"Yes," retorted another. "And add to that a college education and insight, sincerity, and a few other things that go to make up Jane Addams."

Though too modest to enjoy public speaking, Jane did want people to understand about the settlement. Carefully she prepared her speeches, writing ideas on envelopes, on newspaper margins, and stringing the bits of paper over a long darning needle onto a cord knotted at the end. Then she slipped off the papers and shuffled them until the order suited her.

Once when she stood before a group of prominent men and women, they applauded so long that she was embarrassed. Calling her "the greatest woman in Chicago," they said afterwards that her address was "of wonderful strength and quality. It was democracy set to music. . . ." She was thirty-one then, and the settlement had been open only two and a half years. But already important magazines and newspapers were publishing articles about Hull-House and about Miss Addams. It was so right, and she was so right.

Now America felt the vital need of such interpreters of the foreigners and the workers as Jane Addams and her kind. Surging over the ocean from their Old-World farms and villages, immigrants had been coming to the land of the free by the millions and keeping to themselves in the foreign colonies of cities. Some, to be sure, went West to farm, but the free land there was going fast; others hewed timber in the forests or dug coal from the earth. But more and more the cities, growing with giant strides, needed the hard muscles of the immigrant to tend the forges and machines of the Era of Big Business, Big Cities.

Little the rich in their counting houses and the middle-class in their stores knew of these strangers on the back streets. What little they did know was colored with suspicion of these alien hot-blooded Italians, stolid Slavs, and swarthy Jews who now darkened the more familiar immigrant stream of blond Scandinavians. Because such newcomers made up the bulk of the workers, the well-to-do native American had little sympathy for them and said, "Every man for himself," when told of their low wages and injuries in industry. He was apt to forget that his parents or grandparents also had been immigrants. Going was the neighborliness of the small town where a poor man was given a friendly hand and baskets of food. Sharp lines of race and language were beginning to divide the classes from the masses.

Since the Civil War the masters of the Big Business Era had been seizing upon labor as ruthlessly as they had been seizing land, lumber, and ore. But, as they were piling up millions of dollars, the load of landless workers piling up in the cities grew heavier. When hard times took jobs away, these poor had nothing left save a misery that gnawed at the prosperity of the middle classes which also had felt the whip of the masters.

Steadily a feeling was quickening that government must curb the master-capitalists and help the plain people to a decent living. Even before the Civil War, before the Era of Big Business, some champions had spoken and some laws had been passed, but now the murmur was becoming a dull roar. Aroused almost with the moral fervor of the anti-slavery crusade, the great public began an agitation which was to lead year by year to anti-trust acts, a powerful Interstate Commerce Commission, better wages, shorter working hours, less child labor, workmen's compensation, cleaner factories, machinery safeguards, and many another reform.

Jane Addams' calm, firm voice first was heard above the shouting of radicals almost at the outset of this Big Business Era struggle for the rights of the common men, and thousands listened and turned to her as a leader.

12

BIG BROTHER

WELL, ye *ar-re* gr-rowing," said an old settler,
watching men dig a basement for the first of the
many buildings which were to stretch Hull-House over
a whole block.

"Not over quickly, I hope," replied Jane Addams.

"Faith no, ye ar-re deep in th' mud."

He looked at the wallow of Polk Street, about which
a lanky blond young man, the future King Albert of
the Belgians, was to exclaim a few years later while
visiting Hull-House, "We have nothing like this in all
of Belgium."

And Hull-House *was* deep down in the mud, deep
in tears and tiredness, deep in the neighborhood's sins.
It knew the crying of hungry babies and the weariness

of factory workers, and it knew wife-beating husbands
and thieves and murderers. Below the mud, Hull-House
went down, down to the bedrock of fellowship where
all men are brothers.

Settled here, it opened doors to men and women of
many races, many creeds. Perhaps an immigrant family
stood forlornly in the hall, the mother balancing a
bundle on her head and children tugging at her shawl
while the father held out a crumpled paper to Jane Addams. On the paper was written the name of an uncle—
somewhere in the crisscross streets of Chicago. Chicago! The word sounded as strange as a far-away train
whistle, but they could say it—Chicago!

Five years they had been dreaming of it in their poor
village, ever since cousin Tony had come back from
the States wearing store clothes with pockets full of
money, saying proudly, "Now I'm as good as anybody." Across the sea they had traveled and past the
factories and farms of America until the conductor had
thrown open the train door and shouted, "Chicago."

But where in all this city hurly-burly of rushing
crowds and stamping horses, of smoke and strange lan-

guage, could such humble folk as they find anyone to
care what happened now? Who brought them to Hull-
House they scarcely knew, but ah—here was such a
kind lady. She washed the tears from the children's
faces so gently that they smiled back, and soon she
settled them in lodgings near by or at Hull-House until she could seek out the uncle. So she guided them
through the maze of first weeks in the New World—
perhaps to jobs or to classes in English—and whenever
they came back she remembered.

"How do you do, Angelo, how are you getting
along?"

"Fine, Mees Addams, fine. My Joe he work-a een
box fac'try an' go da school nights. I got-a da job een
stock yards. My woman she fine too, an' all-a da keeds.
She come-a da Hull-House soon-a da babee walk."

Just knowing that Hull-House stood back of such
strangers made sharpers keep hands off them, for, as
Jane Addams said, "The settlement is like the big
brother whose mere presence on the playground pro-
tects the little one from bullies."

As one good neighbor aiding another, Jane Addams

sometimes helped her friends get their time-payment furniture out of the collector's grasp, and saved them from being thrown into the street when they could not pay rent. Again, she aided a puzzled laborer to secure his naturalization papers. Or she testified against deserting husbands in the courts which forced them to support their families. Hastily slipping into a coat, Jane Addams often went with a drayman to his stable where a sick horse had to be shot out of mercy, for her word was good with the insurance people. Fearless, she shielded wives from the fists of drunken husbands, or dashed into the midst of street fights to care for wounded men. Word of sickness sent her out quickly with food and medicine, followed perhaps by the Hull-House janitor carrying a mattress.

"I didn't know there were folks like you in the world," an unfortunate man told her.

Always she was so close to her neighbors that she was almost one with them. And they relied on her, knew that she would help them, would go straight to the heart of their problems. Through Hull-House, too, the sick were brought to the county hospital, the poor to charity homes, and the mad to asylums; it was a clearing house for human needs.

One afternoon Jane Addams, carrying a wreath of flowers, entered a tenement room where a pitifully small coffin stood under the crucifix. Children sat on the bed in a clean and solemn row, and the father had his face buried in his hands. Grief-stricken, he turned to her.

"Lucia she was-a my oldes' keed. She was-a fifteen, an' she dead. Een two year she support-a me, but now I mus' work-a five year like-a da dog onteel da nex'-a wans do eet."

Young ones had always worked in the old country, why not in the new? This the neighbors always asked Miss Addams if she told them that the long hours of labor were bad for children and that they ought to be in school. When she explained how standing all day among noisy machines was not so healthful as cutting grain in the sunny fields of Europe, they half understood; but they shrugged and said, in their native tongues, "The kids can speak English and get jobs. We can't."

This was true of some, Jane Addams realized, but not

of many thriving Italian, Bohemian, and German parents who turned their children out to work in order to buy houses and lots. It was a rare father who alone fed and clothed his family. Almost everyone earned—the mother taking in sewing and washing, the sons as "newsies" and bootblacks or, like their sisters, working as factory hands or running ten hours a day in department stores to the cry, "Cash!"

From the iron doors of industry poured boys and girls, already old-faced and toilworn, their soft bones crooked from bending too long over the machines. Mites, just big enough to fold papers, wrapped holiday caramels from early morning until nine at night with nothing for supper but candy, and on Christmas Eve they listlessly refused the Hull-House sweets, saying, "Lookin' at that stuff makes us sick."

Wistful little Angelina, learning English in a Hull-House class, formed her sentence carefully when called upon.

"I get up in the morning and wash my face and then . . ." She halted.

"I," prompted the teacher.

"I sew on pants," she finished triumphantly.

For Angelina it was not, "and then I eat breakfast," but, "and then I sew on pants"—boys' knee pants which she and her mother "finished" for a sweat shop at seven cents a dozen. All day while their needles flew, Mary, aged four, pulled out bastings. Any evening Angelina's worried mother might say, "Put-a da spaghet' een pot. I no stop-a da seweeng. Your pa maybe he have-a no job no more. He say chief let-a da men go. Weenter come-a, he say. Men no deeg-a da deetch."

Down garbage-drenched alleys past basements or up rotting back stairs above saloons in "Poverty Flat" and "The Dive," Jane Addams knew how some of her neighbors were living and working. Windows, closed to keep out the cold, steamed with the breath of stoves and of all the people inside—a mother nursing her baby as she cooked with five little ones underfoot, or a dozen pale tailors and seamstresses stitching and pressing so fast that they hardly spoke in the foul air of a sweat shop. They were sewing perhaps on velvet cloaks lined with fur or on broadcloth dress-suits for the fine folk uptown to wear at the opera, while down the hall or even in the next room somebody lay ill with scarlet fever, or diphtheria, or tuberculosis.

Until late at night, Jane Addams heard the garment workers going home along the street to be back again before dawn in the busy season. They earned four hundred and thirty dollars, more or less, in the eight months of the year when there was work and were always in debt to "the butcher, the grocer, and the pawnshop too."

Before ever Hull-House was started, Jane Addams had felt that labor must unite to win its right to fair wages and fair hours; living here with open eyes and ears had convinced her of it. The common good was what she wanted, but she bent her strength against class warfare.

In the overcrowded, poorly organized clothing industry, sewing went to the one who asked least money; and men, women, and children bidding desperately against each other had forced wages down to starvation, lower than those of any other trade. Because it became known that Hull-House "stood by the working people," the women shirt-makers formed a union here after they had been cut from twenty-five to twelve cents a dozen for making collars and cuffs.

Even with wages falling fast, certain girl cloak-makers refused to meet in rooms above a saloon, but at last they agreed to come to Hull-House. Pertly dressed in bell skirts and high-collared shirt waists with starched bosoms, these American and Irish girls were a vivid contrast to the men they were undercutting, shabby round-shouldered Jewish tailors, sullen with suspicion that Hull-House was a spy for capitalists. Yet these two alien groups, brought together by a common problem, understood each other better after that night when the Woman's Cloak-makers' Union took shape.

Another day, twenty young women on strike from a knitting mill told how they had been unjustly fined for loss of time, and soon Hull-House was able to talk their employer into a fair agreement. In time of strike, such girls realized how feeble they were, on their tiny savings, to hold out against a factory, and so seven of them asked:

"Wouldn't it be fine if we could live together? Then we could help each other out when one of us loses a job or is striking. We're tired of spending our money for horrid rooms and messy things to eat. Nobody cares whether we're dead or alive."

To them, Jane Addams suggested, "Why don't you all take quarters together and try to make them like a real home?"

She paid the first month's rent on a flat and loaned them furnishings, but thereafter this Jane Club financed itself. It gained new members rapidly, but the original girls left one by one to marry. Indeed it was said that more marriages were made at the Jane Club than in Heaven.

For several years now, Jane Addams and Ellen Starr had not been living alone at Hull-House; other young women had been drawn there by the personal charm of the two founders and by the sheer vitality of the settlement itself. Evenings after the neighbors had gone, the residents sat talking over the day's affairs and eating fruit from the corner grocery. The last one to bed had to hang her clothes on the hinge of a door, so crowded was the house.

Julia Lathrop, with her sparkling play of wit and

common sense, was living here and beginning the brilliant career which was to be climaxed in 1912 by appointment as first chief of the federal Children's Bureau; she was a born politician whose Congressman father and John Addams had been close friends. Mary McDowell, in a few years to head the new University of Chicago settlement, taught the Hull-House kindergarten. And Mrs. Florence Kelley, who had inherited the fire and the liberal views of her father, Congressman William ("Pig-Iron") Kelley, was busily investigating the Chicago sweat shops for the Illinois State Bureau of Labor. So such a vital, courageous, keen-minded band of women as the world had rarely seen gathered at Hull-House to fight in the front-line trenches for social justice.

Led by Mrs. Kelley, Hull-House marched down on the sweat shops armed with ugly facts she had laid bare. Because degrading conditions, long suspected, had been proved, Jane Addams felt that Hull-House must step out of the neighborhood and enter politics to help the workers live decently. Miss Addams was no idle dreamer now, but a practical young woman of action.

Piloting Illinois legislators around Chicago, Mrs. Kelley and this committee drew up the provisions for the first factory law in Illinois. Sweat shops were to be cleaned up under this bill, women and girls were to work but eight hours a day, and children under fourteen were not to work at all in factories.

The public soon heard why this measure should be passed. Every night for months, the Hull-House residents talked zealously before meetings in churches, clubs, and union halls, telling what had been discovered —how disease lurked about garments made in infected sweat shops, how tired girls coming home late at night fell into temptation, and how children working in their tender years became stunted little drudges.

Darkly, a bribe was offered Jane Addams; certain men, it was whispered, would give fifty thousand dollars to Hull-House if she would stop exposing the sweat shops. And some once-loyal friends of the settlement began to draw away now that it was no longer merely a harmless day nursery and club house. To all such, Jane Addams had only one brave answer then and in the years to come.

"If we lose one group of friends by certain actions, we shall gain others."

After a winter of "lobbying" in the state capitol by Hull-House residents, prominent Chicago women, and trades unionists, this Workshop and Factories bill at last became a law in 1893. It was but a step forward, but it was a step on the toes of the arrogant masters of industry. Ignoring the fact that other great manufacturing states long had had factory laws, they shouted, "Radicalism! Anarchism!"

Hull-House and Governor John Altgeld were tarred with the same brush. Had not the governor just pardoned three Haymarket anarchists? And now this. Down state, an angry corset manufacturer threatened to put before his factory the sign,

"CLOSED BY THE GOVERNOR OF ILLINOIS"

But Altgeld retorted that he would hang beside it,

"CLOSED TO PROTECT THE CHILDREN OF ILLINOIS"

Hundreds of women relaxed in the leisure of an eight-hour day (until this clause was struck out a year later as unconstitutional); and thousands of children went back to school. As Illinois' first State Factory Inspector, redoubtable Mrs. Kelley was indeed an official to be feared by law-dodgers. Often a sweat shop owner came to Miss Addams to beg her protection from the Kelley vigilance, only to have the explanation, "Mrs. Kelley is not under me. She's working for the state."

But curly-haired Rosie found a way to outwit even Mrs. Kelley. Rosie had been teasing for a certificate saying that she was old enough to work, and one day she swaggered into Hull-House, dressed in her best finery.

"Now I all-a da right, Mees Kelley. You no bodder me n'more."

"How's that, Rosie? What happened?"

"I married now. I went-a da Milwauk', an' now I married ladee."

"But, Rosie, you aren't old enough."

"Yes, I am. Fourteen las' Sunday. Marry las' Sunday. I marry Antonio. He get-a da street-cleanin' job now he got-a da wife."

Speaking on housing reform, which Hull-House now worked toward, Mrs. Kelley described before a large audience a certain block of tenements as "unfit for human habitation." Every two or three rooms held an Italian family and at least one roomer—a half dozen people cooking, sleeping, and trying to live. The buildings crawled with roaches and bedbugs, she said, and reeked with the stench from garbage in the halls and from stables and outside toilets. She omitted nothing, not even the name of the young man who owned them. He promptly stormed over to Hull-House where Miss Addams met him calmly.

"I haven't seen the buildings for some time myself," she said, "and probably you haven't either. Suppose we go over and look at them."

"The place is awful. I know without looking at it again," replied the dismayed young man. "But I haven't owned it very long and do not see what *I* can do. It is the way the people like to live."

"They're very poor, you know, and used to country life in southern Italy. They don't know how to adapt themselves to the crowded city," explained Miss Addams.

"Look here. I'll turn the buildings over to you on a

free lease," he offered on the spur of the moment. "I think that even you can't keep them sanitary very long, but you can do what you like with them."

Hearing of this, a neighbor commented shrewdly, "It takes Mrs. Kelley to stir up the game, but Miss Addams to bag it."

Two or three of the better tenements were sold by Jane Addams and moved off, but the loathsome others were torn down at her order, even though this sacrificed a yearly income for Hull-House of several thousand dollars. Where once the wretched pile had stood was now a playground, the first of a whole system of such recreation centers in Chicago. Children raced, and older folk danced out the rollicking measures of hurdy-gurdies. Thus ran the Hull-House invitation to the playground opening in the merry month of May:

> "There's not a budding boy or girl this day
>   But must be up and help to welcome May.
>   As it fell upon a day
>   In the pleasant month of May,
>   Beasts did leap and birds did sing,
>   Trees did grow and plants did spring."

13

BLACK CITY

Fairy visions of the White City of the World's Fair shifted abruptly to the stark realities of the Black City of Chicago in the depression winter of 1893-4. Once again the ever more complex industrial machine had jammed, and the human cogs had been thrown out of work.

Homeless women found shelter at Hull-House, and idle workmen sat on every chair and bench waiting for word of jobs. The City Hall and the jails festered with men who crept in from the cold, and police kept order among the lines of hungry humans standing hour after hour in rain and snow before relief stations. The poor were kind to each other that miserable winter, sharing their bread and rooms with others more destitute; and

164

Chicago was kind too, giving thousands of dollars to aid.

Bewildered in this crisis, Chicago charity—personified by a benign old man who gave five dollars to anyone who asked—was in need of direction so that the multitude might be fed and clothed. Jane Addams, Julia Lathrop, and Mary McDowell, backed by their rich experience, worked with other civic leaders to bring plan to this confusion by an organization that later became the United Charities of Chicago. So again, Jane Addams was helping to lay the groundwork of the social service structure.

Symbolically, her quiet figure stood that summer against the lurid backdrop of freight cars a-blaze. Strikers were attacking "scabs" trying to run trains, and the nation's railways were in a terrific snarl. The disorder had started when Pullman workers laid down their tools in protest against wage-cuts and lay-offs; then the American Railway Union and allied groups had struck sympathetically. "No violence," warned the Union leader, Eugene Debs, but he was barely heard. Engines were wrecked, men shot—whether by the strikers or the

other side or by ruffian gangs no one was sure. Out-
raged, most Chicagoans took sides, with capital or with
labor; but Jane Addams and others appointed to arbitrate were weighing the right and wrong of both. Day
after day as madness spread, the arbitrators vainly
urged George M. Pullman to talk over peace terms.
Always from his office they had the reply, "The president of the Pullman company holds that there is nothing
to arbitrate."

On the Fourth of July, federal troops marched into
Chicago, under orders from President Grover Cleveland
to protect the mails. Soon the mobs were scattered, the
strike leaders jailed, and even the Pullman men went
back to the shops; but the bitterness of the class struggle
lingered. George Pullman still felt that his employees
had been rankly ungrateful in turning on him; he had
built them a model town with clean streets and neat
homes. But he wanted to carry out his benevolence in
his own way; so he had refused to arbitrate. This the
workers did not forget either.

Saddened by the summer's storm and its lightning
flashes of hate, Jane Addams blamed no one, Pullman

least of all—he had not understood. However, now that she had declared that he was not all right and the workers all wrong—that there was a middle ground—he withdrew his support from Hull-House, and others did too. Still, Jane Addams felt no resentment towards anyone. She grieved that such strife must be, and was discouraged because she had been unable to bring about peaceful arbitration. She had a heavy personal sorrow to bear as well, for her beloved sister Mary, who had mothered her, had died near Chicago on one of those July days.

Early in this troubled year, Jane Addams had applied for the garbage inspectorship of the Nineteenth Ward and had won the post, which paid a thousand dollars annually. Other summers, no smell of roses had drifted about the Near West Side; it had been a stink of garbage rotting as the sun climbed high. Italians had sniffed and said it reminded them of Naples, and children had played store with potato peelings and decayed bananas. The piles of filth, swarming with disease-spreading flies and rats, seldom had been disturbed by the collectors who usually had been drinking beer with the garbage inspector down at the corner saloon. Why should they have heated themselves working? Weren't they all friends of the Alderman?

Disgusted with this bad odor and political laxity, Jane Addams had decided to become garbage inspector herself, aided by a young university woman deputy who tramped the slippery alleys. Soon the high death rate fell, and the Ward was able to take a deep breath. Newspapers made lively comment on Miss Addams' extraordinary new position, and a wit described her as "one of thim reform wimmin, too, that runs a dancin' school up be Polk sthreet and Halsted." Miss Addams' deputy carried on the work for several years until the angry Alderman forced her out of office.

Now a place so big with life as Hull-House could not be ignored, and a mere mention of it over dinner tables anywhere started argument. Girls were "thrilled," but men of the "every-woman's-place-is-in-the-home" type called it queer and dangerous. Parents agreed smugly that you were apt to catch smallpox and other horrible diseases there. To others, Hull-House was simply Miss Addams.

"Land o' livin', ain't there no more o' her?" asked one
old lady.

The neighbors, to whom Hull-House meant the most,
talked the least; it was here, and it was like home, to be
loved but taken for granted. Every week two thousand
Nineteenth Warders came for drawing and cooking,
lectures, gymnasium, clubs, and so on and on.

"Give people what they want, and they'll come."
Jane Addams had spoken truly.

A hundred volunteers gave an afternoon or evening
a week, and the twenty residents, few of them paid and
most earning a living outside, spent nearly all their spare
time in its service. Hull-House had indeed become the
place of which Jane Addams had dreamed, where rich
and poor could learn from each other and where men
and women pale from overstudy could grow vigorous.

In 1895, a curious world read of the settlement in
the book *Hull-House Maps and Papers*, drawn and
written by the residents, one of whom referred to the
miscellany as "The Jumble Book." This same year, too,
saw Hull-House incorporated with Jane Addams as
head resident and prominent citizens as trustees, among

them young Professor John Dewey of the University of Chicago, who already was known as an educator and philosopher. The purposes of the House, as summarized in the charter, were:

"To provide a center for a higher civic and social life, to institute and maintain educational and philanthropic enterprises, and to investigate and improve the conditions in the industrial districts of Chicago."

Six years Hull-House had been open, and in all that time Jane Addams had been away from it no more than a few weeks. In winter, a thousand tasks large and small called her, and in summer she liked to visit from doorstep to step where the neighbors sat gossiping in a babble of tongues.

To her fell more and more the responsibility of running the house and launching its enterprises; for Ellen Starr, now out picketing with strikers, now retiring to the art study and book-binding in which she was an inspired teacher, had not her friend's unruffled calm. In later years she was to withdraw from the world into an Eastern convent. Often impatient with the slow prog-

ress of social betterment and usually seeing a man or a
movement as all good or all bad and not part of each, as
Jane Addams did, Miss Starr once said in her quick way,
"Jane, if the devil himself came riding down Halsted
Street with his tail waving out behind him, you'd say,
'What a beautiful curve he has in his tail!' "

"Well," twinkled Jane Addams, "if he had a beautiful curve in his tail, I hope I should be able to appreciate
it."

The years had been strenuous with financial worries,
endless labor, and discouragements. While many Hull-
House projects were successful, others were short-lived,
such as the coöperative buying of coal. And the neighborhood did not take readily to the purchase of cheap
nourishing food from the Hull-House kitchens, for it
"ruther eat what it ruther."

Learning by doing, Jane Addams had made some mis-
takes. She was still haunted by the memory of a jobless
clerk whom she had encouraged to work digging ditches
in winter; he had caught pneumonia and died.

For six years, Miss Addams had refused time to be
tired or ill. Then a wasting fever left her no choice but

to obey the doctor's order for rest and change. With Miss Mary Rozet Smith, delightful companion of this and future journeys, she sailed for Europe, not as a wistful girl this time but as a woman who had been heard of abroad.

"Miss Addams is better known for her good works and more universally and sincerely beloved than any woman in America," wrote a newspaper editor.

In London she saw many new social ideas being introduced, and in Russia she met the famous novelist and thinker, Count Leo Tolstoy, whom she had admired through his writings. As a simple peasant, he was sharing the work life of the millions, carrying out his belief that the rich should not be supported by the labor of the poor. Somewhat askance, he looked at Jane Addams' modish traveling dress and, pointing at the billowing silk of one of her "leg of mutton" sleeves, said, "There alone is enough goods to clothe a child."

Stimulated by Tolstoy's gospel of the humble life, and feeling that she would understand her neighbors better if she worked at some common task, Jane Addams returned to Chicago determined to bake bread each day.

But the other residents scoffed at this idea as impractical, and she herself found her duties too many to carry out the plan.

Soon she plunged into Nineteenth Ward politics. Once before she had annoyed the Alderman by going over his head to be appointed garbage inspector, and now Hull-House led a fight against his reëlection. With his generous shower of jobs, holiday turkeys, and silver cups for christenings, he had been very popular, even though he was known to be one of the city's big grafters; he had been looked upon as a sort of Robin Hood who robbed the rich to feed the poor. For long the boodler had opposed every effort to make the Ward a better place in which to live, but this was the first time that voters had dared to defy him. Gray pompadour bristling, he warned, "Hull-House will be driven from the Ward, and its leaders forced to shut up shop."

To this threat, Jane Addams merely answered, "We have a lease that does not expire until 1920, and there is no danger of our being disturbed until then."

The Alderman was a crafty foe; he threw reformers out of work, silenced others with ten-dollar bills and kegs of beer, and even tried to bribe Hull-House. Too strong for defeat, he won this and succeeding campaigns.

Even the youngsters knew about the political warfare, and one said, "Boodlers puts rotten bottoms to cedar block pavin'."

Being good citizens was a game for the boys and girls in the Hull-House Clean City Club who scrambled around after school in gutters picking up waste paper and burning it. Carmella found the most—a thousand pieces—and was crowned May Queen amid a court of girls dancing with wild flowers in their hair.

Jane Addams had been particularly anxious to bring good government into the Nineteenth Ward in order to show American democracy at its best to new citizens and to immigrants who had fled the tyranny of Old-World rulers. Some were Russian revolutionaries who had escaped dramatically from Siberian prisons. Certain of the foreigners in Chicago and elsewhere were anarchists; that is, they believed that people would be happier if government were utterly abolished. For the most part, the anarchists were peaceful, intelligent men; but a few were violent, talking of bomb-throwing and assassination to win their ends. The actions of these unbalanced few had made the very word "anarchist" dreaded in the United States when news swept out from Buffalo that President William McKinley had been shot by a half-crazed Pole.

"A plot to overthrow the government! Hunt down the anarchists!" the vengeful public cried after the assassin had confessed to a creed of anarchy.

On the Sunday morning following the Buffalo tragedy, Jane Addams and Raymond Robbins, from another settlement, hurried to Chicago's mayor to urge upon him fair play for the anarchists seized in the city—the right of bail, the right of attorney, the chance to prove their guilt or innocence. No damning evidence had been ferreted out against them, no conspiracy.

"At this crisis, you best can show that justice in the United States is fair to all and does not break down under stress. What better answer to every social agitator?" they asked him.

The mayor replied that he dared do nothing yet toward even-handed justice, but that he would pass them through police lines to the prisoners. Here in his dark cell, Jane Addams visited a terrified editor who beseeched her, "What of my wife and daughter?" And she talked to other radicals, all scholarly men shocked at the attack upon the President, anarchists in philosophy but not in deed.

"This is like Russia," they told her wretchedly. "They put you behind bars here too for speaking and writing what you think."

Within a few days, she was able to get them out on bail. Wrathfully, the public saw her acts as defiance, not as valiance, and accused, "You encourage anarchism." A newspaper remembered then that Prince Peter Kropotkin had stayed at Hull-House briefly a few years past and had talked there—more proof of Hull-House anarchy! What the newspaper forgot to add was that this great philosophical Russian anarchist also had lectured before eminent Chicago societies and at several universities.

Only a few people cared to understand why Jane Addams sought justice now, as always, for the "underdog." She and others eye to eye with her saw that men twisted by fetid centuries of Old-World oppression could grow straight again in the new country only in the fresh air of free speech, free press, and equality before the law.

14

"ITS DOORS ARE OPENED WIDE"

A S THE seasons came and went, Halsted Street knew
spring's muddy waters, summer's beating heat, the
dust-winds of fall, and winter's slush. Far out in prairie
and woodland, trees were budding, grain was ripening,
red leaves scurried, and snow fell white. To the east
Lake Michigan changed from gray to blue to green, an
inland sea. But of all the beauties of nature, Halsted
Street saw only the arch of the sky and, over roof-tops,
the fire of the setting sun. Vaudeville posters and wash
lines were its scenery.

Children were growing up who had never seen a lake
or walked in a woods or picked a flower. When Hull-
House first took them to various summer camps in the
country, they touched the grass to be sure it was real,

or lay stomach-down watching the curious ant people. Boys who were not afraid of the "cops" fled in terror from cows, and shivered at night when an owl hooted. After two amazing weeks, they came back, plump and tanned and eyes big with a hope for next year.

"Dis vere you put der name down vor vresh air?"

"Can I go out-a da vacash too?"

Early in the spring the children started asking, anxious to plan. Even if a girl didn't own a nightgown, she thought she must wear a white silk dress and carry a suitcase to "vacation."

"I got no slippers like der odder kids," little Jewish Fanny whispered to a Hull-House lady, looking down at her old scuffed boots. "I don' wanna go."

"You just come along with me," ordered the grown-up.

Together they walked to a large department store on Twelfth Street where ecstatic Fanny chose a shiny pair of buckled patent leathers and wore them right out of the shop. Every night at Holiday House on Lake Geneva she slept in them between those wonderful cool sheets—why, she'd never slept in *sheets* before! Years later, when Fanny was a leader of Chicago fashion and had an exclusive dress shop, she boated over from a millionaire's Geneva estate to see again this spot she had remembered even in her success.

Through all the dreary days, older folk held in their minds bright pictures of the homeland and in their hearts a longing for the smell of earth and trees after rain. With a sigh, they told the children of holiday music and dances, of the old churches, and flowers everywhere. Tiny Francesca, who had thus heard much of Italy, entered Hull-House for the first time and, sensing its charm, asked her father, "Dees-a da Itàlia?"

An Italian woman, who had been passing her narrow years between market-stall and cookstove, stopped in wonder before a bowl of velvety red roses on a Hull-House table.

"Ha, da rosa! She come-a from da Itàlia?"

Never before in America had she seen roses, though florists' windows a mile away were lush with them.

To the worshipful Italians Miss Addams was a saint walking the earth, Saint Jane, and her house was "la

Casa di Dio," the House of God. Thus with religious
fervor they must pour forth their adoration.

Was this the woman who had been called godless by
ministers and priests because no creedal religion was
taught at Hull-House, this woman who followed so
closely the teachings of Christ by loving the humble?
With her deep wisdom, she knew that any one creed
would drive away many in sore want. Catholics, Jews,
Protestants—all must be welcome.

> "A house stands on a busy street,
> Its doors are opened wide,"

sang the Hull-House Woman's Club, knowing well
what those words meant.

Through Hull-House passed junk dealers and pro-
fessors, capitalists and fruit vendors, scrub-women and
society folk, mayors and policemen, saloon keepers and
English reformers—the famous, the infamous, and the
unknown. To all of these Jane Addams talked with the
same courtesy, perhaps answering their ring at the door
herself. The person interested her, not the reputation.
She invited old women for a holiday from the poor farm

and arranged a dinner to celebrate an Irish wedding anniversary.

With his bride, dynamic young James Ramsay MacDonald, fluent of tongue and flashing of eye, visited at Hull-House; he was to be Great Britain's first Labor prime minister. Some years later another Britisher, the illustrious John Galsworthy, was so charmed with a Hull-House presentation of his play that he gave the settlement permission to use any of his dramas without charge. On Theodore Roosevelt's arrival, the Boys' Club band performed with ear-splitting enthusiasm and was overjoyed at his genial request for more. After this, there was no doubt in any boy's mind as to who was Vice President of the United States, though one Jewish urchin stubbornly insisted on calling him, "Theodore Rosenfeld."

If, in the Old-World way, foreign guests at Hull-House left shoes outside their bedroom doors, Jane Addams shined them and never gave herself away when the departing visitor left a tip for the "bootblack." Humorously, she declared her intention of writing an essay on *Famous People Whose Boots I Have Blacked.*

"ITS DOORS ARE OPENED WIDE"

"I like Miss Addams because she don't put on side," said a lad earnestly. "She don't act better than me."

On Halsted Street, as on all other streets the world over, Youth beat against the bars of dullness—eager to laugh, to dance, to be gay—and past sober jailers it rushed down to carnival and merry-go-round. Tossing hats in air, Youth shouted, "Strike up the band," while flabby men and painted women leered from side-shows. As always, elders tore their hair in anguish over Youth's wild fling.

But on Halsted Street, an ocean stretched between Youth and Maturity, for Youth was American and Maturity was Old-World. Cocksure with its American dress and slang, Youth was ashamed of its parents who spoke broken English and wore foreign-looking clothes. It scorned to obey the father as head of the family and to "give in" the pay envelope to the mother on Saturday nights.

"They don't know nothin'," Youth would say, powdering its cheeks or slicking its hair for the dance.

Italians, who tried to seclude their daughters until

the father should find husbands, grieved if a fair zitella ran away to marry the boy she loved. And honest Bohemian and German parents, taking all their children's earnings, wrung their hands when a shop-girl daughter stole Easter finery, or a son robbed his employer's till for show money—"dose good-for-nodings."

"Why don't you let your girls come over to Hull-House and have a good time?" Jane Addams asked the Italians. "They want to go out in the evenings like the Americans, you know."

And to the Germans and Bohemians she tried to explain why the young should be allowed a little freedom with their wages, "A girl needs a pretty blouse and a flower for her hat sometimes, and any boy wants to take his sweetheart to the theater and buy her ice cream afterwards."

But that Youth might honor the traditions of its fathers and not alone all things American, Jane Addams celebrated at Hull-House the holidays and heroes of many countries, and she started a Labor Museum. A gnarled old father telling how he had fought with Garibaldi's "Red Shirts" to unite Italy, or a shy mother spinning and weaving so deftly on the museum's spindles and looms, won new respect from their children. The Old-World craftsmen worked in iron and brass, too, and with wood, carving wondrous angels, or with clay, shaping by hand the curves of vases—such beauty might a section-hand or a tailor or a scrub-woman create, re-membering. Seeing this skill and tracing, by museum displays and photographs, the rise from such simple hand-crafts of the machines with which they worked every day, the young sensed dimly the age-long story of in-dustry and their kinship with the past. Yes, they might know the new ways, but their fathers knew the old.

Because it was more fun to go to a Hull-House dance than to a tawdry ballroom, jollier to be in a Hull-House play than to watch cheap vaudeville, the young folk made it their own "Palace of Delight." As pirates and gypsies, they flirted at masquerades; and sometimes they tinkled tambourines in a tarantella, kicked their heels to wild Russian music, or stomped out an American square dance with *Pop Goes the Weasel*.

Now and again, they acted melodramas with mus-tachioed villains and swooning heroines, but more often they played Shakespeare, liking to strut their hour upon the stage as lords and ladies and to make love and die in golden verse. Even the eight- and twelve-year-olds learned "yards and yards" of Shakespeare, and one Jewish tyke who flitted about, as Ariel, years after saw his name in the lights of Broadway. Another boy, who took part in Hull-House drama and dancing from the age of four, became the chief male dancer at Milan's great Scala Theater.

One day Jane Addams came upon a small girl peering into the empty theater with wondering blue eyes.

"Is this where the fairy princess lives?" asked the child.

No play was given carelessly; for weeks and months it must be rehearsed to bring glory to the actors. After a fierce debate and many motions moved and seconded, the fourteen members of the Lincoln Club, all Jewish and all under eighteen, launched into *Merry Wives of Windsor*. Coming through snow and rain on Saturday nights, few missed play practice—not the lads who worked until six as clerks and office boys, nor the girl stenographers and bookkeepers who kept the Jewish

186

Sabbath. Until eleven the company rehearsed and then had a supper cooked in "kosher" style. Into midnight they argued politics, evolution, and literature; all read newspapers and serious books, and some studied law at night, meaning "to be somebody."

Slowly, the old farce came to mirthful life. Sadie Goldman *was* giddy Mistress Page, and Ikie Rosenberg, stuffed with pillows, *was* jovial Falstaff. Some gorgeous costumes were loaned by artists—slashed velvet doublets, jeweled swords, and pointed shoes for the boys, and for the girls unspeakable delights. Mistress Page wore a mink-collared robe of cloth-of-gold over a coral satin petticoat, with a veil fluttering down from her peaked medieval cap to her topaz necklace. That other minx, Mistress Ford, pranced in sables and blue brocaded satin girdled with paste emeralds and pearls. Awkwardly, the players basted together other costumes, using denim and faded velvet or whatever else they could buy with eighteen dollars and seventy-three cents.

"Golly, we don't want to put on long socks and short pants. We're bowlegged." Boys scorned the trunk hose.

"You have to. Look at the costume book," chorused the rest.

"Can't I wear my new dress with the hand-embroidered waist?" a girl pleaded.

"It wouldn't fit in the Middle Ages," again the cast shouted. "Everything must be just right."

After six months of rehearsal, they played at last before an audience, small because of a March blizzard. Actors tripped over scenery, and Falstaff just missed losing his beard, but none forgot their lines. It was a triumph.

"They laughed, they laughed!" cried Mistress Ford, quivering with delight.

There were other boys and girls who listened to the siren voice of the great city calling them from drab duty to "flip" rides on trains, or steal glittering baubles, or "borrow" horses and buggies. If they were caught, the law shut them in jail where they awaited trial and punishment—children as young as eleven—with safe-crackers, pickpockets, and streetwalkers giving them lessons in vice. So was it in Chicago before the world's first Juvenile Court was opened in 1899. Miss Julia

Lathrop and Hull-House, lawyers and club-women, had worked for this measure to shield youth.

Henceforward, the state became an understanding father to its erring children, not anxious to punish but to talk over problems and try to straighten out the bad twists. Now young folk were not held in jails or police stations but in a home-like old residence where they had to take off their shoes before going to bed. Ashamed to admit petty crimes, the boys usually said they were in "for killin' a Chinaman."

Other states speedily followed the lead of Illinois, for they too realized a situation which Denver's juvenile judge Ben Lindsey expressed dramatically:

"It would be much worse to take a wayward child to some of the jails in which I have seen them steeped in corruption, as the first step to correct their faults, than to take your sick child to the city garbage dump and leave it abandoned, alone, and unattended."

15

RED, BLUE, AND GREEN

Around the block, Hull-House was spreading in brick buildings of the Old English type. But within its heart was still "t'ole Hull house" and within the core of this was Jane Addams' study, "the octagon," an eight-sided room built by the early owner. Swirling rounds of mellow glass shielded the upper halves of "the octagon's" tall windows, and crisp curtains fluttered out below towards the courtyard lawn and shrubs, now green, now brown with the seasons. On the walls hung pictures that Jane Addams loved—a view of Toynbee Hall, and photographs of her father and her friends.

Here in "the octagon" she wrote on social subjects, dictated letters to her secretary, talked to a shawled widow about her taxes, and answered the telephone a dozen times a day. The cook came in to plan the evening dinner, and the engineer to say he must order coal for the furnaces and lighting plant. All in one, Jane Addams was the author with a tender glowing touch, the efficient and practical executive, and the neighbor who impulsively gave her own fur-lined cape to a shivering Scotchwoman and then was so human as to regret it afterwards.

Said the Irish of Miss Addams, "Sur-re, if there's annywan'll have rayspict in their bur-ryin's it's her. Sur-re, it's her that's gr-reat—gr-reat f'r a woman."

Close above Jane Addams' desk upon the wall were bright patches of color—stripes of red and squares of blue, zigzags of green. These were carefully drawn maps of the neighborhood, blocked off by nationalities.

Where the red showed, there lived the Jews, some still with the fear of persecution in their eyes, patriarchs seamed with sorrow. Far away in Russia, one gentle Talmud scholar had heard of Hull-House, and like the symbol of a Promised Land it had seemed to him; so he had brought his family to Chicago. Straight and tall his sons and daughters were now growing, reaching out for the riches of the settlement; in the closed book of the future, one was to be a symphony musician, another to teach at a great university, and a third to be an able lawyer.

Marked by vivid blue were colonies of Italians, moved often by whole villages from the Old World, gustily drinking their wines and eating their spaghetti and sausages. Though they gossiped among themselves, they did not talk too much lest they betray some secret that would bring swift revenge. Superstitious Antonios and Antonias wore charms around their necks and put tinkling bells and tufts of fur upon their peddlers' carts to keep away the Evil Eye. And wrinkled hags concocted love potions, or shaped wax into the figure of an enemy and stuck pins into the feet, the belly, the head to torture him.

"Da magic he no cross-a da wat' nice-a," they grumbled when the intended victim's health continued good.

A brawny policeman, his face the map of Ireland, owned this too. "Sur-re, an' there be fairies in Oireland, but they can't live over-r here," he said wistfully, telling how the Little People used to throw potatoes in the fire and sour the milk and pinch the pigs until they squealed.

Green splotches upon the Hull-House charts revealed the houses and tenements of the Irish who held themselves above the Italians. Scornfully, they had passed on the lowly work they once had done—digging ditches and laying track—to the "wops" who had not been in America so long, and they now were making their quick-witted way into "white-collar" jobs as teachers, politicians, and lawyers.

Moving farther west to trees and yards when times were good, moving back when they were hard, going up and going down, Germans, Poles, and all the rest were trying to get along. Of a sudden, olive splashed among the map colors, signaling the arrival of the Greeks. Round about in one year, a thousand appeared, mostly men without wives, Hellenic shepherds turned tradesmen so shrewd that Halsted Street began to say, "It takes a Greek to beat a Jew."

By hundreds, Hull-House taught them English

through clever pantomime and through primers in which railroads were substituted for rats and cats. Proud of their race and boasting of "the Athens," the Greeks came. In the gymnasium they showed their age-old skill in wrestling and in the theater, the grandeur of ancient Greece. Before crowds from the Gold Coast and the Nineteenth Ward, they played *The Return of Odysseus*, Odysseus himself in rags and the rest in tunics copied from old Greek vases. By day they were shoe menders and peddlers of fruit and ice-cream, but on these nights they became heroic figures.

Blowing in homesick strain upon their shepherds' pipes, they gathered on street corners of a Greek holiday, wearing short pleated white skirts and embroidered jackets. From Greece also, they brought the reverent procession on Good Friday midnight when, past stores and houses draped in purple, they marched from the Greek church by candlelight, chanting hymns beside the sepulcher of Christ. Irish policemen held back the throngs of emotional Italians, crossing themselves, and of the curious Jews, and of the other peoples in this Little Europe.

194

RED, BLUE, AND GREEN

With strong reds and blues, greens and olives, Hull-House drew the pattern of the district, and from Monday to Sunday saw it at its best and worst. Though side by side, few of these races lived in complete friendliness; often their suspicion grew into enmity. Taught from babyhood to hate Turkey, which held part of old Greece, patriotic Greek lads attacked young Turks on sight. And when Hull-House discovered with a shock that Italian anarchists had rented its auditorium to celebrate the assassination of King Humbert of Italy, Greek men bared stout arms and said, "We'll fight them for you."

Going to the country for a summer holiday with a Hull-House group, certain shabby Italian girls scowled at the prettily dressed Jews and in jealousy dumped all Sophie's frocks out of her suitcase, punched Rachel's hats, tied Rebecca's coat in knots, and hid Goldie's big glass beads.

"Oh, a-a-a-oh," screamed the Jewish girls, seeing the mess. "Those dagoes have done ut. Wait'll they catch ut." And they ran to tell the director, a wise woman of big and understanding heart, who said, "The Italians are envious of your nice clothes, and that's why they were so mean. Some of them are very poor."

Three days later, when Japanese lanterns had been strung from the trees for a party, Sophie let Carmella wear her best ruffled dress, and Goldie gave her pink organdy to Violetta.

The next summer, as the boys were planning an overnight hike, sturdy Benito blurted out, "We don' want Abe t' go 'long. He acks smart, an' he's a-scared t' fight. Da beeg sissy—he wears-a da bat'robe."

Under his breath, Benito muttered to his gang, "I don' like-a dat sheeny Abe, an' I'm gonna knife 'm."

The wise woman asked, "You don't like Abe, do you, Benito? You think he's a coward because he won't fight. But just look at your muscle! Who wouldn't be afraid of you? Why don't you teach Abe how to use his fists?"

And she cornered Abe too. "You're afraid of Benito. Why?"

"Oh, he's so rough, an' he swears, an' always wants t' fight."

"Be honest, Abe. You think you're better than he is.

Don't you? You talk better English, you have better suits, and you're in a higher grade. But that's because your mother and father work hard, and give you a good home and clothes, and keep you in school."

Abe reddened and tried to back away, but she held him. "Don't forget that many Italian boys have no fathers, and that their mothers have to go out working. They have nowhere to play but in alleys with tough gangs. Do you wonder that they swear and act rough and have poor clothes?

"Now, I don't approve of fighting, but I do think that every boy should be able to defend himself. Why don't you make friends with Benito? And keep on wearing your bathrobe. Don't toady to him."

At supper, she happened to tell the true story of the Italian and the Jewish girls. Next day, Abe and Benito walked arm in arm.

Like a lighthouse among the surging waves of immigrants stood Hull-House, beaten by storms but always keeping afire the beacon of idealism and fellowship that attracted ardent young people year after year. William

Jennings Bryan's daughter Ruth, dark-haired and attractive at nineteen, breezed through the house; and Frances Perkins, tired of being a home girl, came from Massachusetts and served Jane Addams without pay as an investigator. Miss Perkins was a few years out of Mount Holyoke College where she had been called "Loquacious Linguist." Wearing sturdy clothes, she tramped through Chicago tenements collecting data, and then went back East to continue the distinguished career of public service which was to place her in President Franklin D. Roosevelt's cabinet as Secretary of Labor. During this same Roosevelt administration, Ruth Bryan, now become Mrs. Ruth Bryan Owen and an ex-Congresswoman from Florida, was to go to Denmark, the first woman ever named a United States Minister.

When a jolly crowd set forth on bicycles for a picnic along the north shore, youthful Mr. Swope's strong legs pedaled before him "on a bicycle built for two" Jane Addams, or Ellen Starr, or, perhaps, the girl he was to marry. At Hull-House, Gerard Swope, future head of the great General Electric Company, got his

first insight into labor problems. Another future industrial leader, Walter Gifford, who was to be president of
American Telephone and Telegraph, stayed at Hull-
House; and W. L. Mackenzie King, eventual premier
of Canada, was also among the scores of young men
and women who, in the years, worked enthusiastically
for the settlement and carried far afield its idealism and
its practical ways of meeting social issues.

Authors and engineers, business men and teachers,
farmers and artists, doctors and lawyers, and social
workers—almost every kind of person who goes to
make up the world—lived in Hull-House at one time
or another. Some brought their wives and children after
apartments were added to the block.

Dr. Alice Hamilton, one of the first specialists in
occupational and industrial diseases; Miss Sophonisba
Breckinridge, trainer of social workers; Miss Edith
Abbott, later the dean of the School of Social Service
Administration at the University of Chicago; her sister
Miss Grace Abbott, head of the Immigrants' Protective
League, who was to follow Miss Lathrop as chief of the
United States Children's Bureau; and many other dis-

tinguished women were on the illustrious roll of Hull-House residents, living together—often for many years—and exchanging ideas, agreeing and disagreeing, but never divided by petty quarrels.

Graciously Jane Addams presided at her table, and diplomatically she settled arguments among her comrades, never dictating but only suggesting. Freedom was allowed each to go his own way, speak his own mind, but always chivalrously, never meanly. Hull-House was Jane Addams' home; it *was* Jane Addams. When she was gone, it was like a house with the mother away, somehow strange. Not until she returned did everyone again feel comfortable and easy. She knew where every bit of furniture was and every picture, often moving them about like any home-keeper, tugging at a couch herself, or calling, "Please, Mr. or Miss ——, *you* can help me."

Among the residents were an Old Guard and a Young Guard, or a Noble Set and a Frivolous Set. The Old Guard was made up of mature men and women seriously engaged in their careers, but never so sedately that they could not laugh at the antics of the Young Guard, or Frivolous Set, which chased over roofs at Hare-and-Hounds.

"Do they marry?" asked a visitor breathlessly.

"Often, alas, often," she was told.

When a fire broke out near by, the Frivolous Set stayed up half the night serving coffee and sandwiches to the firemen. Or for weeks before St. Patrick's Day, it would be making favors and planning gorgeous effects for the Irish dance. Every day at Hull-House was a rare adventure for the Young Guard fresh from college, fresh as paint. Impudently and with high hilarity, the Frivolous Set "took off" the Noble at parlor plays, and once sang a jingle beginning,

"When everything is clean and neat,
Miss Addams changes pictures."

And it was the Young Guard that hiked about until Christmas Eve was morning, distributing little trees and big baskets of food, clothing, and toys. With children tucked in bed, mothers scrubbed floors and laid down clean newspapers to prepare for this American Christmas. In many an Italian home, candles burned about the lowly manger of the Christ Child and the bright plaster Wise Men kneeling in the straw before Him. The flames wavered when the Santa Claus from Hull-House opened the door softly, and they flickered again when he stole away with a low, "Merry Christmas."

Six Irish youngsters slept in one bed, three at the top and three at the bottom, and on a near-by cot three more left room for the mother when she should return at midnight from washing dishes in a downtown restaurant. All in a row, nine stockings hung from the kitchen shelf, nine stockings with holes for toes and holes for heels. Noiselessly, the Hull-House Santa Claus tried to fill up the holes with oranges and apples. On top he stuffed dolls and horns and chocolate mice, and then went away, feeling himself a smart fellow.

16

AMERICA'S JOAN OF ARC

IN THE crush of a banquet given for Theodore Roosevelt at an exclusive Chicago club, Jane Addams lost her hat and had to go home bare-headed. Next day, the club sent her a check for fifty dollars with which to buy a new hat. She returned the money, writing, "Enclosed please find your check for fifty dollars. The hat I lost cost only ten dollars, and I was wearing it the second season."

Several months later Jane Addams went downtown to second the nomination of Theodore Roosevelt as President of the United States. She stood on the platform of Chicago's Coliseum and ringingly addressed the convention of the new National Progressive party which, in this summer of 1912, had broken away from the ranks of "stand-pat" Republicans. An audience of ten thousand cheered her to hoarseness as she closed and stepped down to lead a parade of suffragists waving the yellow banners of "Votes for Women."

From the streets of her neighborhood, Jane Addams had gone forth into city and state to urge legislation for the workers; now she entered the national arena. Woman Suffrage was only one reason why she stumped the country that fall for the new party and for dynamic Theodore Roosevelt, whose outspoken liberality she sincerely admired. It was also because—among other reforms—such as those designed to bring government close to the people—the Progressives stood behind what she and others like her had been striving to achieve through the years:

A living wage for all.

No child labor.

An eight-hour day.

Sickness, unemployment, and old age insurance.

Safeguards against industrial accidents.

Workmen's compensation.

This did the Progressives ask of Big Business, that it

be a source of life and strength and not of fear and injury and even of death.

Campaigning north and south, east and west, Jane Addams was escorted to auditoriums by torchlight parades of enthusiastic men and women. She spoke without oratory, sincerely and forcefully, swaying her hearers with the vision of social justice held by the new party. The rallies ended in a tumult of cheers, a blaze of red bandannas marked with the party symbol, "the Bull Moose," and a jubilant singing of patriotic airs by Jane Addams Choruses.

On Election Night in November, telephone and telegraph wires hummed with returns that were hastily chalked up on newspaper bulletin boards and printed in headlines. "Extray! extry! all-abou'-the-'lecshun, extry!" shouted newsboys over the land. By next morning, the Progressives knew that—although they had won over the conservative Republican candidate, William Howard Taft—they had been beaten by the Democrats and Woodrow Wilson.

None the less, the spirited Progressive campaign had set people to talking about social problems and corruption in business and politics. Once again it was proved that reforms which seem radical today are the legislation of tomorrow, for many of the planks in the Progressive platform were pulled up one by one and nailed into state and federal laws.

To be sure, Jane Addams was criticized for her Progressive politics. "It's a shame to identify that woman with any partisanship," said a New Yorker. "She's broad enough to stand for the good in every man's platform."

Some declared that she and others of her sterling mettle had unknowingly been tools for politicians who wanted the campaign to appear a crusade. Her direct action had always stirred up antagonisms. In the early days of factory legislation, and again in her tilt with the Nineteenth Ward boss, and yet again when she went bail for the anarchists after the McKinley assassination, she had been jeered at as, "Anarchist! Radical!"

Among the great army who loved her, there had always been enemies throwing spears at this American Joan of Arc who had fought against city slums and sweat shops. Often she had been wounded, but to de-

feat or victory she must follow the banner of her convictions, be true to herself and what she knew of life.
It was only this unflinching courage that saw her
through the dark days of the World War when—
"black-listed" by patriotic organizations, called "Pacifist," and generally derided—she came out for peace
negotiations with a bravery that even her foes admired.

Born into Quaker ideals and so into a love of peace,
Jane Addams had besides a broad sense of internation-
alism come from living so long in a foreign quarter.
Few Americans knew so well the hearts of Europeans.
She had seen them hoping for their children, struggling
toward the stars; and now they were to be crushed
under the heels of military leaders going on to glory.
Beneath the surface discord, she felt the essential
brotherhood of the common man. This was the spirit of
Hull-House that she tried to carry abroad into a world
at war. Such a mission was inevitable for a woman of
her deep sympathy and understanding.

In the fall of 1914, street cars clanged busily along
Halsted Street, and merchants fitted girls to school

shoes, boys to their first long trousers. Yellow squares
of light in many windows showed families around supper tables, and people shuffled up and down the well-
worn Hull-House steps. Familiarly, the clock on the
neighboring church tolled the hours of the night over
sleeping heads, but uneasiness walked abroad like a black
cat. Far away in Europe, the blood kin of the Irish and
Russians of Halsted Street were fighting the blood kin
of the Germans.

With the spring, Jane Addams answered a call to
preside over the International Congress of Women at
The Hague. Across the gray Atlantic the Dutch liner
carrying her and other American delegates steamed
without event, but in the English Channel it was stopped
for three days by British authority which feared that
the women's conference on peace would weaken soldier
courage. Only two hours before the opening of the
Congress, the Americans landed in Holland and hastened toward The Hague through fields of red and
yellow tulips. Facing ridicule and opposition, fifteen
hundred brave women from neutral and warring nations
assembled to pose the heart-felt question: "Why can't

the issues of this war be settled by negotiation rather than by bloodshed?"

They asked not that the war cease on the instant but that outstanding neutral scientists and lawyers, business men, economists, and sociologists meet continuously and offer proposals to the warriors which might end battle. Out of this might rise an international association that would act, without war, to free oppressed peoples, give certain countries seaports, and share more equally the riches of mine and soil. Possibly all nations would eventually cast aside their arms and settle their difficulties peacefully as did each one of the United States.

Appointed by The Hague Congress, Jane Addams and a Dutch doctor carried the suggestion for a Conference of Neutrals to the war capitals of Europe; another delegation visited the neutral nations. In Berlin, Vienna, Paris, and London, they heard troops marching and saw widows and crippled soldiers praying under the arches of beautiful cathedrals. Everywhere, Jane Addams and her companion talked to chieftains of state, grave men who replied in substance: "We are fighting in self-defense. To sue for peace negotiations would mean that we are weak. But perhaps, if a conference of neutrals made certain proposals to us, we would be glad to listen. Perhaps . . ."

Woodrow Wilson, the great neutral to whom the world looked for leadership, felt that the time was not yet ripe for calling neutral heads together. Still in the first year of war, still sure of their strength, the military powers were not ready for peace terms; nor did they care to listen when, a year and a half later, President Wilson spoke of "peace without victory."

It was as though the world were watching two powerful mastiffs snarling at each other's throats. It was as though Jane Addams and other peace leaders wanted to throw the cold water of reason upon the fighters to calm their rage, and as though the crowd cried, "No! They must battle until one is whipped, or else they will pounce every time they meet."

When governments made no move toward bringing peace, Henry Ford, the American millionaire and builder of automobiles, chartered a "Peace Ship." Accompanied by peace pilgrims and newspaper correspondents, he sensationally set forth for Europe in December 1915 with the slogan, "Get the boys out of the trenches by Christmas." He wished to set up an international center where peace problems might be discussed and from which a Conference of Neutrals would be developed. With serious misgiving but with a desperate hope that some good might come of it, Jane Addams had agreed to go on the "Peace Ship," but she suddenly fell so ill that she was sent to a hospital for six weeks. However, her name was linked with the over-idealistic and failing enterprise, and she heard the jeering laughter of the world.

Though Hull-House residents stood loyally by Jane Addams herself, many disagreed with her ideas and were for out-and-out war. Never had there been any knee-scraping at the settlement, and there was none now. When the Boys' Club band assembled to march in a Preparedness parade, someone cried, "They ought to be stopped!"

But Jane Addams replied evenly, "Let them go. If they believe in Preparedness, they are expressing their convictions."

After the United States declared war against Germany and Austria, Hull-House young men enlisted in the army, not waiting for the draft, and the older residents valiantly "did their bit." Often khaki-clad youths from the neighborhood left farewell dinners at Hull-House and the embrace of wives and sweethearts for overseas. In canning, knitting, and rolling of bandages, the district's foreigners were in marching step with other women throughout the land. Chicago, sixth largest German city in the world, discovered that it had needlessly feared an angry boiling over of "the melting-pot."

Jane Addams herself talked for the Food Administration, whose catchwords of "Hooverizing" and "wheatless and meatless days" became known to the smallest school child. She would do her share toward feeding the hungry in peace or war. However, not every town cared to hear her—a Pacifist!

Once the howling dogs of war were kenneled, a spirit of international good will surged into the hearts of men, fresh as the spring turning green the bloody hunting-grounds. The League of Nations was established in the hope of deciding future quarrels by arbitration, of reducing arms, and of studying war causes.

After those years of war bitterness, there came a day in December of 1931. Jane Addams was lying on a hospital bed in Baltimore, ready for a serious operation, when word arrived that she had won the Nobel Peace prize. Not fifteen years before, people and press had scorned her, but now they sang her glory. She had not changed her views one whit and had been spreading ideals of peace as president of the Woman's International League for Peace and Freedom.

With Dr. Nicholas Murray Butler, president of Columbia University and long a peace general, Jane Addams shared the year's award of about thirty thousand dollars. She gave her half to the Woman's International League which had been organized following The Hague Congress and had active groups in most countries of the world.

The Nobel recognition pleased Jane Addams deeply, not because it added fame but because it showed that the world's people were again shaking hands. All along the way, when universities had honored her with degrees and when many other shining medals of acclaim had been hers, she had taken them not for herself, but for her ideals of fair play and understanding among men.

Of recent years, in voting on the great, Europe and America always place the name of "America's uncrowned queen" high on the list. This is testimonial to the high courage, far-seeing wisdom, and rich humanity of a woman who has never hesitated to champion causes she believes right, never hesitated to share their unpopularity through forlorn days.

Long ago, in her college valedictory, the girl Jane Addams had said:

"The opening of the ages has long been waiting for this type of womanhood. . . . Now is the time for a faint realization of this type, with her faculties clear and acute, from the study of science, and with her hand upon the magnetic chain of humanity. . . ."

Nearly a half century has passed since the young Jane Addams went to live at Hull-House, but her friendship is still as warm and her memory as fresh as when she took the first baby from a tired mother. In the early years, Hull-House nursed the sick and fed the poor, watched over immigrants and wayward youth, tried to answer every need. But the burden of human want was so heavy in Chicago and other metropolises that groups acted to meet special necessities, and slowly social work became a science.

Many cities paralleled Chicago's Juvenile Court, Juvenile Protective Association, and Immigrants' Protective League; and Chicago followed other centers in its United Charities, Visiting Nurses' Association, and many another institution. Universities began to train youth for social work and investigation, while, awakened by such interpreters of the poor and the foreign as Jane Addams and her kind, the masters of capital gave millions for human betterment.

In this far-reaching movement of modern times, Jane Addams has been a heroic figure; she is one of the great pioneers who have blazed a trail through the wilderness of needs and greeds. No one has done more than she to open a vast territory of social service to young people of today who long—as the girl Jane Addams longed—to aid the poor and luckless.

17
HULL-HOUSE TODAY

Proudly wearing new clothes given by a rich uncle, a Greek boy struts to the Hull-House reception desk with his brother and says, "I'm Alex, an' this's Nick. I'm eight, an' he's seven, an' we're twins."

Outside in the hall, Italian bootblacks scramble for business. "Hey, mister, ya need a shine." And, "Lookit, he give me a dime, an' ma'll buy meat fer us." Or, "J'on'y make two cents, Gyp? 'At's good dough."

Every week from fall to spring, a small town's population comes to Hull-House—six thousand boys and girls, men and women. Seventy-five residents have rooms or apartments here, and a hundred and fifty volunteers give several hours a week, feeling amply repaid by glimpses into the patient and picturesque lives of the neighbors. The thirteen buildings cover a block, housing also other organizations for social welfare; and, near the shores of Lake Michigan, the settlement has a green and gracious estate, Bowen Country Club. Once Hull-House had an annual budget of two thousand dollars, but now it must spend over a hundred thousand dollars every year.

As a tall oak grows from a little acorn so Hull-House has grown, reaching roots down to the bedrock of fellowship where all men are brothers. Its branches are firmly twined into Chicago tradition, a tradition of neighborliness which the great roaring city of pork and railways and skyscrapers has not forgotten in acquiring over three million people.

Visitors from far away have heard of the House and, thronging in, stare curiously about and are stared at by the youngsters. Impish Camilla asks, "What're they lookin' at? What's funny about us? I'll make a face at 'm." And she does.

"Don't you remember that lady we met in the country? She knew about Hull-House and said she'd like to see it. I guess these are some more people like her," explains Ameriga who is sixteen and has curling hair and lovely dark eyes.

Quite simply, Jane Addams served Queen Marie of Rumania with tea at one of the black tables in the Coffee House, and as simply she invites a Hindu princess or an American college girl to dine. Perhaps she is resting in an antique rocker when a tourist rushes over.

"You're Miss Addams, aren't you? I knew from your pictures. I've admired you so much. I wanted to tell you . . ."

"That's very kind of you, I'm sure," says Miss Addams with a warm handclasp.

Hull-House is still Jane Addams' home; it *is* Jane Addams in charm and hospitality. She arranges fresh flowers about mantels and book-cases, ties summer covers on the chairs, and has the hand-woven table runners washed. The sunshine falls caressingly over polished brasses and the sheen of old mahogany and walnut, or lights upon a green vase big enough to hold one of the Forty Thieves in *Ali Baba*. About these mellow furnishings hangs many a tale. In a dark corner is the portrait of a little girl, hair a tangle of ringlets and face like a dusky flower from her native Italy. Sometimes a well-dressed woman walks up to this picture followed by eager children who cry, "There's ma when she was a kid. Ain't she pretty?"

Another painting, of a young mother nursing her baby in a simple kitchen with the window open to the blue Italian sky, has filled many a peasant heart with yearning. One day a woman old in trouble looked up and saw.

"Madre di Dio, eet ees me!" she shrieked. "Me an' dat son who ees een jail. Soch a sweet babee he was. Soch a sweet babee.

"Long time ago een Itàlia da artist ladee painted. Soch a sweet babee!"

Eastward from Hull-House beyond shabby streets the city's towers rise like the shining dreams of men. Closer are alleys twisting past the back doors of saloons and underworld hide-outs. It is easy to walk down the alleys. Will Youth care to reach the towers?

Even in good times, a boy has to push himself to find

an honest job, and in bad times he just stops looking. He gets tired of standing around with no "cuters" (quarters) in his pockets. Maybe he starts thinking of his father and asking what hard work ever did for "the old man."

Perhaps the lad and his gang already have robbed slot machines or broken into vacant houses, hacked away the lead plumbing, and sold it for movie money. Or the boy has wistfully eyed the candy bars in a grocery store but could not buy any unless . . . The shrewd slattern who ran the store waddled up to him and whispered, "You get me the auto tire. Yes? I give you all the candy you eat. Yes?"

Older youths are ready to teach the "greaseballs" (greenhorns) of thirteen and fourteen how to jiggle a car until the loosened wheels fall off, or how to drive away the "hot shot" almost under the owner's nose. Easy money this is, and often bloody money too. Once, when youngsters refused to strip autos for the older "guys" and ran off, all escaped but one who hid in an ash-can. Enraged, a "hoodlum" of nineteen emptied his revolver into the tin, and the boy rolled out dying. But the "hood" was put "on the spot," and, shortly after, his body was found in an alley.

From car stealing, the crime students graduate into street hold-ups with a "rod" (gun), and then into pay-roll robberies and safe-cracking. If they show promise, an organized band takes them over, and they are in the "big racket" so long as they keep out of "the stir" (jail).

"If ya get caught stealin', I'll lick tha hide off ya," some fathers say to their sons.

Perchance the father is himself a "twister," or an uncle is a gangster flashing diamonds and rolls of green-backs. Always crime offers thrilling and dangerous careers to poor boys. Sometimes falling in love makes a youth want "to go straight," or possibly, after being in prison for six months, he comes out saying, "Useta t'ink I knew ever't'ing when I was sixteen, but now 'm nine-teen an' dunno s'much. Makes ya feel good inside ta go on the legit."

Maybe a boy just gets so hardened that he stops at nothing, listens to nobody. Sadly, honest foreign parents regard these reckless youngsters who fancy themselves Americans and scorn obedience to an Old-World father. Families are always moving to better districts in a desperate effort to get their lads away from evil company, and once a factory superintendent shot his own son rather than see him a criminal.

Hull-House faces squarely the fact that neighborhood boys have a much better chance to go down than up. If they are in trouble, it coöperates with the Juvenile Court and the Juvenile Protective Association to set them right. It gets jobs for them and takes them to the country; and it is a club-house where they can box, play pool and basketball, and go to dances. Here also they meet young men who have grown up hereabout but are not "hoodlums," young men who have worked their way through college. There's Rocco of the agile mind and body who's a pharmacist downtown and, at the same time, is one of the cleverest basketball players in Chicago. Big, deep-voiced Pete, so handsome he has a bevy of girls around him at dances, used to run with "toughs," but now he is a lawyer in the Loop.

Seeing how "regular fellows" live, some of the youngsters get the idea that is a good way to live. So slowly that he scarcely knows it, a boy may come to think that winning a basketball game is just as exciting as stealing a car, or discover that he hasn't any "stuff" for boxing if he stays out all night and smokes cigarettes.

More closely held by family tradition, the girls of Halsted Street are not wild. After grade-school, they usually go into a factory until they marry at eighteen or nineteen. The marriage is a glorious affair with the smiling bride in white satin and a veil of lace, and the proud groom in a tuxedo rented from the same store. And ah, the cake! Tiers upon tiers of white pastry are wonderfully frosted with birds and flowers, and at the top is Cupid. On time, the happy couple buys an upholstered parlor set and a gleaming stove—these they must have. They love the babies as they come, and the bigger ones take care of the small, rollicking on the floor with the dog.

Such a future any Hull-House girl expects to have, but she has not yet forgotten the grim winter of 1931 when, driven breakfastless from home by a father ugly with worry, she tramped the soles out of her shoes seeking work. In despair, she turned to Hull-House which gave her such a meal as she had not tasted in months and paid her a dollar a morning for sewing under an expert tailoress. She made clothes for herself and pants with hip-pockets for her brothers, coats for the babies, and all manner of garments for the neighborhood needy. Well-dressed and well-fed, she went forth in the afternoons and, God willing, found a job.

18

ROUND THE YEAR

IT IS Spring Exhibit time in May, and long-legged girls are "toting" visitors about Hull-House. The girl guides are wearing yellow linen jumpers they have made themselves with sheer white organdy blouses; someone has already nicknamed them "the Canaries." When a newspaper photographer arrives, Miss Addams calls the proud "Canaries" around her for a group picture.

In the mellow dining room, with its beamed ceiling and its huge platters of Syrian brass and Flemish pewter, its bowls of purple iris and yellow snapdragons, a small child with a blue ribbon tied to her red curls is gravely tuning her violin. She starts on a wrong note but the rest is charming, and the audience chatters applause. Then a boy with his fingers perspiring on the piano keys gets stuck in the middle of *Hungarian March*. Other performers sit in the front row, hotly awaiting their turns to play and sing for Miss Addams and for mothers and fathers.

Across an alley, the year's pottery is on display—a magnificent prancing horse, bull-fighters, the fiesta. Here also are scarlet plates and cups that girls have made for their own party. Broad-shouldered Miguel, who sold ice cream in Mexico and never worked with clay before coming to Hull-House, is rolling out cactus spines with his big fingers and sticking them to a clay stalk; he is a skillful potter and has won national recognition. Ten-year-old Angelina has devoutly molded a slimly lovely figure of St. Therese and a font for holy water, a child of four has shaped an orange mug with bumps on it, and the blue sail-boat and red giraffe are Manuel's, aged eleven.

Upon the walls are pictures alive with color and action—Little Black Sambo, pirates, a Spaniard making love, Halsted Street, factory stacks, Hawaiian dancers, and on through the vivid imaginations of the children

who painted them. One Italian family is so artistic that
it spends most evenings around its kitchen table,
drawing.

A dark-skinned Mexican boy, wearing a belt of red
and blue woven by himself, is leading his old mother
from the pottery and painting into the weaving room
where patient hands at many looms have fashioned
scarves and rugs and luncheon sets, each with the fresh
beauty that only hand-work has. Soft spring winds
through this place of arts and crafts shuffle poetry
leaflets on a table. Children and grown-ups have composed the verses and illustrated them with wood-cuts
which have been printed in the Hull-House shop by
classes of boys.

Though twelve-year-old Patsy Panico would rather
play the accordion, he has written in free verse:

THE BUTCHER

Here is the butcher
Chopping off the chicken's head
With a big chopper
Squak, squak—says the chicken
On the other side of the room is

Half a cow
The pig is hanging by his tail
He was killed yesterday
My mother will buy half of him
And we will make sausages.

THE JUNGLE

Broken houses
Here and there
Pipes for chimneys.
Their houses are made of boxes
And broken-down wagons,
With no windows
At all.
They live in a big, empty
Lot
With factories closed
Or they would work in them;
Bums,
Beggars,
Hoodlums,
Tramps,
But they're
Only workmen
Without any
Work.

Patsy's chum Daniel Rizzo, a dreamy Italian lad, is afraid of storms:

> Waves dashing over the boat
> Suddenly a storm
> Comes up knocking the yacht over almost
> Almost drowned I see
> Mountains and trees
> Trees shaking.

Strong-muscled John Giacaloni can "sock a homer" any time, but, at thirteen, he doesn't think poetry is "sissy":

THE RAGMAN

> He pulls and pulls his wagon every day
> In the street
> The rags and old paper man.
> Have you any papers?
> Have you any rags to sell?
> I sometimes help to push the wagon
> Any old paper?
> Any old rags to sell?
> Any old macaroni boxes?

THE KNIFE GRINDER

The knife grinder is always
In back of my father's store.
Every Thursday
He is in back of the door.
He says "knives to grind"—
Sometimes I say, "No"
He tells me,
"Watch me;
Maybe you will learn
And work with me"
The sparks disappear
Into his eyes;
There is a big can
Of water in front of him;
There is a wheel
Where he grinds his knives.

When you are up in a skyscraper looking down, you
feel a certain way, says John Grasolina:

When I am up here
I feel gay and blue
The trains stop and go
The smoke makes me choke
And the building black

Up so high I am
I think I am in an airplane
Thirty two floors above the people
The people look like bugs.

Frances Bissios is thirteen and a leader in her club; this
is her poem *Hallowe'en:*

It was a very black night,
We saw not a creature.
The cornstalks and pumpkins
Hid every feature.
A cat howled loudly
Which scared us a bit,
Shapes took form oddly
Then lanterns were lit,
Which cheered us a bit.

Over at the Boys' Club on this Spring Exhibit day are
freshly washed pets tended by their anxious masters in
tennis shoes and ragged caps. Even the neighborhood's
toughest boy "Kinks" has his hair slicked down and is
wearing a clean shirt. Dogs howl, cats yowl, and everybody shouts with excitement. A turtle nips at a poodle's
nose, and a police dog with a blue bow on his collar

hungrily eyes a pink-eared rabbit and a white rat. Fluffy yellow chicks twitter in a box on the ping-pong table, and a calico kitten fights and scratches. One tiny tyke, pulling at the safety pins that hold his torn jersey, is sad because his father wouldn't let him bring his pet pig.

The Harlequins are playing Shakespeare's *Much Ado About Nothing* and forgetting that their wigs are hot and their costumes heavy in the sultry spring night. "Act Well Your Part. There All the Honor Lies," is the motto over the Hull-House stage. Sometimes, above the din of Halsted Street cars and the strumming of a Mexican orchestra across the way over a Greek butcher shop, the audience cannot hear what the actors are saying.

Bulky women light on their feet are whirling each other over the floor of Bowen Hall, and a few men are brave enough to dance the Irish jig and the waltz. With *Home, Sweet Home* they leave, calling, "Come to see us this summer," after this last neighborhood party until fall.

Through the day, Jane Addams has been hostess in

this her home, Hull-House. She has greeted hundreds of folk at tea; and at dinner, when the Coffee House was crowded, she has helped the waiters carry in food and clear tables. More than one man exclaimed, "Miss Addams brought me my pie!" Not until ten o'clock do the residents finally persuade her to taxi away for a quiet night on the Near North Side. As she goes, she turns, saying characteristically, "See that everyone is comfortable and finds his way to the theater. And then *do* go to bed yourselves."

By the week-end, clubs of young people are packing for a house party at lovely Bowen Country Club. Birches and shooting stars climb up the steep sides of ravines, violets stud the grass, and purple lilacs hedge beds of red tulips—all spring is here. Mrs. Joseph T. Bowen, member of an old Chicago family, gave these acres at Waukegan's edge to Hull-House twenty years ago; now on them, besides an old farmhouse, are cottages yellow as butter, a dining hall, Goodfellow Hall for charades and dancing, and a boys' camp.

"I'm not afraid to die if Heaven's anything like Bowen Country Club," once said a dying lad.

In the blue swimming pool, girls do a mermaid dance, and flower petals drift. "Chili" is serving to "Little Eva" on the tennis court and boasting, "I'll take your money."

"It's in the bank," "Little Eva" yells back.

Young married couples with smartly dressed children drive out to the grounds in shiny autos. They have prospered and moved from Halsted Street to the suburbs, but they grew up in Hull-House clubs and still belong—perhaps their romances began at Bowen. Now the full moon is drawing other boys and girls out to walk the woodland paths, "picking wild flowers" they call it.

When summer sizzles down on the West Side, tanned merry-makers in bathing suits under pajamas and over-alls board street cars for a day at the beach. Licking ice-cream cones, half-naked children swarm in and out of hallways past baby carriages, dogs, and last winter's overshoes. Italian women glide to the bakery with trays of bread dough balanced on their heads, and urchins with heads shaved for the summer shoot dice on the sidewalks or brag to each other, "Da rats in our alley 'r fatter'n in yers."

Down at the Maxwell Street market, live poultry flutters and squawks, but the glistening eels and big-scaled carp smell a long time dead. Gamins dart through the crowd upsetting fruit carts, snatching purses, and tweaking the eagle feathers of an Indian medicine man selling snake oil.

"Bargain day, lady, for vifteen zents you get a classy dress," a merchant tries to pull the shopper into his store under hanging bunches of garlic.

"Red hots, red hots, de're hot. Don' let 'em get cold," shouts a vendor.

In the long twilight, everybody makes a parlor of the front steps and the street. Cold water spurts from open fire hydrants, and gleeful youngsters sail boats in the gutters. Men sleek with sweat fill milk bottles with the water and pour it on thirsty morning glories in window boxes and on scraps of yard growing yellow-hatted sun-flowers and drowsy four-o'-clocks, squash vines, and even corn. Two boys on cracker boxes and two on gaso-line cans sit playing cards. When the street carnival's ferris wheel begins to turn and the merry-go-round to play *Barney Google*, all the young world yells for nickels.

To these folk of Halsted Street, advertisements for summer excursions to the north woods or through the Great Lakes are just so much waste paper. All the same, a thousand have two weeks of vacation that seems just as delightful as a trip abroad; they go to Bowen Country Club. This is the first train journey for many who sit tensely on the edges of green plush seats. Swiftly, they travel past chuffing locomotives and lines of yellow freight cars and past Chicago's back-stairs into a glamorous world that is strange to them—the fashionable North Shore of pretty girls in floppy hats and youths in white flannels.

Bowen has only a few rules: "You must be happy" (that's easy to obey); "Don't pick the flowers"; and "Keep off the highway" (No, you *can't* run over to the golf course and look for balls).

Days and nights are restful for weary mothers and high with adventure for the young. Mistaking a wasps' nest for some funny kind of football, a smart city boy kicks it. Off the diving board jumps a girl all arms and legs. "Socko!" Another freckle-face hits a "homer" for her baseball team, and a crippled child finds a "fairy ring" of toadstools. Long after the evening dancing or marshmallow roast, "Curly" lies in bed, whispering secrets to her best friend who occupies the cot next to her own.

"I'm reducin' because Joe says I'm too fat. Imagine your fella tellin' you that!"

"Huh-uh. . . . Uh-huh." Giggles.

All summer long people come and go, knowing for two weeks a simple, gracious, joyful way of life. At home, the Scarlatas and the Apostolatoses eat off the kitchen oilcloth or perhaps grab food from the stove, but here they are served at tables set with colored doilies and flowers, pretty glass and china. And they have all they can eat; on "seconds" and "thirds," hungry young-sters gain five or ten pounds. Rachel, who by her ste-nography helps to support a large family, alertly notes down all, for she is to be married soon and does want her things nice. She will have sheets on her bed as at Bowen and not sleep in blankets as at home, and surely they can afford such simple furniture and cretonne curtains.

"Anyway, we're not going to buy a lot of ugly trash," she writes her sweetheart.

When the gypsies leave the open road and again loll in Halsted Street doorways, rags and gold ear-rings bright as their flashing smiles, and when the "lady students of the Orient" who "speak seven languages" are back telling fortunes, they are sure signs of fall. Round and about is perhaps the largest winter colony of these wanderers in America. Strange and wild, gypsy children flit through Hull-House, and sometimes far away are heard the mad, sad violins at a Romany wedding dance.

Nobody kicks the fiery gypsies about, but the gentle Mexicans—they are the "under-dogs." Of all the poor houses, theirs are the poorest, and in not a few the father must sleep with a gun under his head to shoot the night-prowling rats. When hard times come, they are the first to be laid off; it has always been so with the latest immigrants.

Like all the other strangers who, in the years, have started on the long climb toward becoming Americans, the Mexicans find Hull-House a friend in need. Here they can learn English and so stand a better chance of jobs. And Hull-House revives their drooping pride by having them use their wonderful primitive sense of color and design in pottery, weaving, and drawing.

One night thirty Mexicans from a near-by mission, among them a blind man and a baby in a carriage, came into a settlement pottery class of Chicago artists. They could not speak English, but they could watch the teacher's hands and so learn what to do—all but the baby who sucked quietly on his bottle, and the blind man whose wife explained in Spanish. Swiftly they modeled rows of perfect pots. In astonishment, one of the artists exclaimed, "Do you mean to tell me that they have never before handled potter's clay?"

"No," replied the teacher, Mrs. Myrtle French, head of the Ceramic department at Chicago's Art Institute.

"Well, I guess *we* had better give up. I've been trying all evening to get some shape to this mess."

Now that the Jews, Irish, and Germans, with their hungrily eager minds, have largely moved away, Hull-House has shifted from lectures and college-extension courses toward the arts and crafts in which Mexicans and Italians are so adept. They earn money by their work, for Hull-House sells it in a fascinating boulevard shop and also ships ceramic ware all over the country. A pottery factory, Hull-House Kilns, is directed by Mrs. French and her husband, and operated by a young Italian with the head of a faun who gave up prize fighting for art.

Not even a chimney fire or a baseball game keep jaunty little Vito away from the clay that grows under his nimble fingers into city scenes. Such a piece as an officer directing traffic sells readily; the policeman is far larger than the autos but none too big to express the boy's admiration. Prancing in one night, Vito says, "N'evenin', Missus French. I've brought t'whole bunch."

And he has—his father, two aunts, and brothers, sisters, and cousins. With professional pride he demonstrates how the clay is molded and glazed.

"Ya see," he tells Mrs. French, "I told 'em to come along, an' I'd show 'em I could make pott'ry an' sell ut. Dey t'ought I was stealin' alla cash I bring home."

As the year rolls around to December, Hull-House is filled with the Christmas-has-come-again smell of evergreens. Big brothers carry legginged midgets up stairs to the theater for the Christmas play, *Pinocchio.* Hand in hand as always, five Mexican sisters are ten great black eyes under five scarlet tams. Dante, who has been sent home to wash his face, comes back with red-cheeked Penelope who is so plump that she must eat half the honey-pastries from her father's bakery. Nobody is supposed to see the play without a ticket, and the lady at the door knows that the saucy boys in patched shirts are lying when they say "Please, da dog ate up muh tickut," or, "A big guy swiped ut." But she lets them in just the same.

After the play, Santa Claus jovially gives out candy, and along the line goes the whisper, "Who's Santy dis year—Sam 'r Chris?"

Over in the Music School, twelve-year-old Rebecca practices so hard for her own piano recital that her shining black braids jig up and down; she composes music too. Not long ago her family, with a blind father, was ragged and woebegone, but now, since knowing Hull-

House, it is neatly darned and ambitious; a son is even trying to go through college.

For the 'cello and the singing which are her life's only joys, a pale Russian girl with twisted back walks a mile after selling dresses all day. Young Mrs. Rosenberg and her dimpled daughter, whose father has just given her a wrist-watch for fine playing of Mozart, are other music students. When a girl herself, the mother used to shirk her scales and gave small promise of the brilliant pianist she has since become. In the hours of perfecting the difficult concerto with which she is to solo in a Woman's Symphony Orchestra concert, Mrs. Rosenberg has to desert her careful housekeeping, but her proud husband says, "It's all right if you give me beans. I know you can cook."

Up some stairs at Hull-House, men at billiards take measured aim, while through the walls come the rat-a-tat of fists on a punching bag and the hoots of boys watching their "dancing mothers." A señorita of seventeen is at work on her trousseau in the room next to a Citizenship class; she calls to mind the saying of her own Mexico: "Surely St. Peter must have opened the gates of Heaven to let down such a beautiful damsel."

More familiar to Halsted Street than robins' song are the cheerful hurdy-gurdies in the spring. It is the season of St. Joseph feasts when richer Italians feed the poor, and of Good Friday's solemn churches, and of the glorious Easter. Perhaps a little later comes the Greek Easter, and for its feasting are black-nosed lambs, and kids with pointed faces, and red eggs stuffed in wheaten loaves.

If a girl has nothing but broken shoes and old winter clothes to wear, she will not now come to dancing school on Saturday. Whether she is chubby and yellow-haired or stringy and dark, she has to have a new dress fresh as spring, with anklets to match. This Hull-House knows so well that it bathes the poorest girls and decks them out prettily for the afternoon. Then, once again, it is Spring Exhibit time, and another year ends and begins on the same day.

People may come and go, and times may change, but Hull-House lives on. In words, perhaps, the settlement hears small thanks, but it expects none. Once, when an ardent volunteer complained that a woman for whom she had done much was not even grateful, Jane Addams replied in that ringing, girlish voice of hers, "Was that why you helped her? For thanks?"

To the thousands who have almost grown up in Hull-House, it is as much a part of their lives as school and church, and they bring their children back and their children's children. Hull-House is like home, and Jane Addams is like a mother who will always love them no matter what they do.

"America's Joan of Arc" she has been called, and "America's Uncrowned Queen," but the title that suits her best is simply Jane Addams of Hull-House.

ACKNOWLEDGMENTS

THE AUTHOR is deeply indebted to Miss Jane Addams for her assistance in this work through interviews, through consultation on the manuscript itself, and through permission to use material selected from her published books and articles, from her college essays and orations, and from letters written during her European travels (1883-5, 1887-8).

The author also owes much to friends of the Addams family, including Miss Mary Fry, Doctor Thompson, and Jacob Sill, all of Cedarville, and to Miss Flora Guiteau and Miss Ann Barton of Freeport, Illinois. Mrs. Kenneth Knowlton, now living in the Addams Cedarville home, coöperated most graciously in the search for material, and Miss Alta Saxby of Freeport gave much local color about the region.

Data on Rockford Seminary days was contributed

ACKNOWLEDGMENTS

in letters from Miss Addams' class-mates, including Miss
Elizabeth Smith of DePere, Wisconsin; Miss Maria
Nutting of Berkeley, California; Mrs. Eleanor Froth-
ingham Haworth of Washington, D. C.; Mrs. Mattie
Thomas Greene of Urbana, Illinois; Miss Mary Agnes
Baker of Denver, Colorado; and Mrs. Harriet Wells
Hobler of Bronxville, New York. Mrs. Catherine
Waugh McCulloch of Evanston, Illinois, took time from
her busy day as a lawyer for a most informative inter-
view on the Seminary of long ago.

On Hull-House and its activities, from early days to
the present, the residents—many of long standing—gave
generously of their reminiscences and knowledge. Espe-
cially must be mentioned Miss Enella Benedict, Mrs.
James Britton, Miss Edith de Nancrede, Miss Gertrude
Smith, Mrs. Myrtle French, Miss Norah Hamilton,
Miss Nina Kenagy, Miss Thora Lund, Miss Adelene
Titsworth, Mr. Leon Garland, Mr. Bert Boerner, Mr.
Frank Keyser, Mr. Eri Hulbert, Mr. Robert Morss
Lovett, and Mr. George Hooker. The author is also
grateful for material to officials of the Immigrants' Pro-
tective League and the Juvenile Protective Association,

ACKNOWLEDGMENTS

and to Mr. Marquis Alderman, of the latter, for permission to visit neighborhood homes with him. The manuscript also contains data on the neighborhood derived from personal observation, for the author has done volunteer work at Hull-House.

BIBLIOGRAPHY

THE FOLLOWING books, newspapers, magazines, and pamphlets were consulted in the course of research:

Abbott, Edith, *Immigration: Select Documents and Case Records* (University of Chicago Press, 1924)

Abbott, Grace, "A Study of the Greeks in Chicago" (*The American Journal of Sociology, November 1909*)

Addams, Jane, "The Art Work Done by Hull-House, Chicago" (*The Forum, July 1895*)

Addams, Jane, "The Bad Boy of the Street" (*Ladies' Home Journal, October 1909*)

Addams, Jane, *Democracy and Social Ethics* (Macmillan, 1902)

Addams, Jane, *The Excellent Becomes the Permanent* (Macmillan, 1932)

Addams, Jane, "Founders' Day Address" (*Friends Intelligencer, November 5, 1932*)

Addams, Jane, "Foreign-Born Pupils in the Primary" (*The School Journal, August 14, 1897*)

Addams, Jane, "Hull-House, Chicago: An Effort Toward Social Democracy" (*The Forum, October 1892*)

Addams, Jane, "Jane Addams's Own Story of Her Work" (*Ladies' Home Journal, March-May, 1906*)

Addams, Jane, *The Long Road of Woman's Memory* (Macmillan, 1916)

BIBLIOGRAPHY

Addams, Jane, "A Modern Lear" (*The Survey, November 2,* *1912*)

Addams, Jane, "The Objective Value of a Social Settlement" (in *Philanthropy and Social Progress,* Crowell, 1893)

Addams, Jane, *Peace and Bread in Time of War* (Macmillan, 1922)

Addams, Jane, "The Revolt Against War" (*The Survey, July* *17, 1915*)

Addams, Jane, *Second Twenty Years at Hull-House* (Macmillan, 1930)

Addams, Jane, *The Spirit of Youth and the City Streets* (Macmillan, 1909)

Addams, Jane, "The Subjective Necessity for Social Settlements" (in *Philanthropy and Social Progress,* Crowell, 1893)

Addams, Jane, *Twenty Years at Hull-House* (Macmillan, 1910)

Addams, Jane, "Why Girls Go Wrong" (*Ladies' Home Journal, September 1907*)

Addams, Jane, "With the Masses" (*The Advance, February 18,* *1892*)

Allen, Devere, *Adventurous Americans,* edited by Mr. Allen (Farrar, 1932)

American College Girl (Page, 1930)

Annual Catalogue of the Officers and Students of Rockford Seminary (issues *1876-81*)

Arena Magazine (*September-October 1901*)

Baker, Ray S., "Hull-House and the Ward Boss" (*The Outlook, March 26, 1898*)

Barnard, Eunice Fuller, "Jane Addams: Bold Crusader for Peace" (*New York Times Magazine, December 20, 1931*)

Beard, Charles A., *Century of Progress,* edited by Mr. Beard (Harper, 1933)

Beard, Charles A., and Beard, Mary R., *The Rise of American Civilization* (2 vols., Macmillan, 1927)

BIBLIOGRAPHY

Beer, Thomas, *The Mauve Decade* (Knopf, 1926)

Besant, Walter, *East London* (Chatto and Windus, 1901)

Binford, Jessie F., "Understanding the Delinquent" (*1931 Year Book, The National Probation Association*)

Booth, Charles, *Labour and Life of the People*, edited by Mr. Booth (Williams and Norgate, 1889)

Bourget, Paul, *Outre-Mer Impressions of America* (Scribner's, 1895)

Bowen, Louise de Koven, *Growing Up with a City* (Macmillan, 1926)

Brodlique, Eva H., "A Toynbee Hall Experiment in Chicago" (*The Chautauquan, September 1890*)

Bryan, Mary Baird, and Bryan, William Jennings, *The Memoirs of William Jennings Bryan* (Winston, 1925)

Campbell, Helen C., "The Jane Club and Its Meaning" (*The Interior, September 17, 1903*)

The Centennial Eagle (Centennial Eagle Company, 1876)

Chicago Tribune, August 4-8, 1912; May 11, 1930

The Child, the Clinic, and the Court (New Republic, 1925)

Current Literature, "The Only Saint America Has Produced" (*April 1906*); "Jane Addams: The Lady of the Melting Pot" (*August 1910*)

Darwin, Charles, *The Descent of Man* (Appleton, 1888)

Darwin, Charles, *On the Origin of Species* (Murray, 1859)

Dewey, Davis R., *National Problems 1885-97* (The American Nation: A History, vol. 24, Harper, 1907)

John Dewey, the Man and His Philosophy (Harvard University Press, 1930)

Essays of the Graduating Class ("News" Steam Press, 1881)

Ferris, Helen, *When I Was a Girl*, edited by Miss Ferris (Macmillan, 1930)

Freeport Bulletin (*issues of 1860-71*)

Freeport's Lincoln (Lincoln-Douglas Society, 1929)

Freeport Weekly Journal (*issues of 1860-80*)

BIBLIOGRAPHY

Gale, Zona, "Great Ladies of Chicago" (*The Survey, February 1, 1932*)

Godey's Lady's Book (issues of 1868, 1871, 1877, 1881)

Hackett, Francis, "Hull-House—A Souvenir" (*The Survey, June 1, 1925*)

Hamilton, Alice, "At the War Capitols" (*The Survey, August 7, 1915*)

Hannig, Amalie, "Christmas at Hull-House" (*Ladies' Home Journal, December 1911*)

Hard, William, "Chicago's Five Maiden Aunts" (*American Magazine, September 1906*)

Harper's Weekly (issues of 1867, 1870, 1875)

Henderson, Archibald, *Contemporary Immortals* (Appleton, 1930)

Hendrick, Burton J., *The Age of Big Business* (Chronicles of America Series, vol. 39, Yale, 1919)

The History of Stephenson County, Illinois (Chicago Western Historical Society, 1880)

Howland, Harold, *Theodore Roosevelt and His Times* (Chronicles of America Series, vol. 47, Yale, 1921)

Hull-House bulletins (Hull-House, January 1891; March 1892; February 1894; 1899; 1901; 1902; 1903

Hull-House Maps and Papers, written by Residents of Hull-House (Crowell, 1895)

Hull-House Year Book (Hull-House, forty-second year; forty-fifth year)

Jenison, Madge C., "A Hull House Play" (*Atlantic Monthly, July 1906*)

Johnston, William J., *Sketches of the History of Stephenson County, Illinois* (Burnside, 1854)

Jones, Anita Edgar, "Mexican Colonies in Chicago" (*The Social Service Review, December 1928*)

Jones, Katherine A., "The Working Girls of Chicago" (*Review of Reviews*, American, *September 1891*)

BIBLIOGRAPHY

Josephson, Matthew, *The Robber Barons* (Harcourt, 1934)

Kelley, Florence, *The Working Child* (1896)

Kellogg, Paul U., "Twice Twenty Years at Hull-House" (*The Survey, June 15, 1930*)

Kirkland, Joseph, "Among the Poor in Chicago" (*Scribner's Magazine, July 1892*)

Lathrop, George P., *Spanish Vistas* (Harper, 1883)

Lewis, Lloyd, and Smith, Henry Justin, *Chicago* (Harcourt, 1929)

Linn, James Weber, "Introducing Jane Addams" (*University of Chicago Magazine, November 1933*)

Literary Digest (*December 26, 1931*)

Lord, Russell, "Madame Secretary" (*The New Yorker, September 2, 1933*)

Miller, Alice, "The Hull-House" (*The Charities Review, February 1892*)

Montague, Francis C., *Arnold Toynbee* (Johns Hopkins, 1889)

Moore, Dorothea, "A Day at Hull-House" (*American Journal of Sociology, March 1897*)

The Nation, "Jane Addams" (*February 3, 1916*)

New York Sun (*September 27, 1912*)

North American Review (*September-October 1901*)

Olcott, Charles S., *The Life of William McKinley* (Houghton, 1916)

The Open Court (*February 1892*)

Orth, Samuel P., *Our Foreigners* (Chronicles of America Series, vol. 35, Yale, 1920)

Parrington, Vernon L., *The Beginnings of Critical Realism in America 1860-1920* (Harcourt, 1930)

Peattie, Elia M., "Miss Jane Addams" (*Harper's Bazaar, October 1904*)

Pierce, Bessie L., *As Others See Chicago*, edited by Miss Pierce (University of Chicago, 1933)

BIBLIOGRAPHY

Pierce, Fred C., *Picturesque and Descriptive History of the City of Rockford* (Daily Gazette, 1887)

Pooley, W. V., *The Settlement of Illinois from 1830-50* (University of Wisconsin, 1908)

Porter, Mary H., "A Home on Halsted Street" (*The Advance, July 11, 1889*)

Ralph, Julian, "Chicago's Gentle Side" (*Harper's New Monthly Magazine, July 1893*)

Reckless, Walter C., and Smith, Mapheus, *Juvenile Delinquency* (McGraw-Hill, 1932)

Review of Reviews (American), "The Civic Life of Chicago" (*August 1893*); (*September 1912*)

The Rockford Seminary Magazine (*issues 1877-81*)

Rosenberger, Jesse Leonard, *In Pennsylvania-German Land* (University of Chicago, 1929)

Ross, Edward Alsworth, *The Old World in the New* (Century, 1914)

Rugg, Harold O., *An Introduction to American Civilization* (Rugg Social-Science Course, vol. 1, Ginn, 1929)

Sandburg, Carl, *Abraham Lincoln: The Prairie Years* (2 vols., Harcourt, 1926)

Steiner, Edward A., *On the Trail of the Immigrant* (Revell, 1906)

Stone, Melville E., "The Higher Life of Chicago" (*The Outlook, February 22, 1896*)

The Survey (*July 10, 17; August 7, 1915*)

Taylor, Graham, "Jane Addams—Interpreter" (*Review of Reviews, December 1909*)

Taylor, Graham, "Jane Addams' Twenty Years of Industrial Democracy" (*The Survey, December 3, 1910*)

Teller, Charlotte, "Miss Jane Addams of Hull-House" (*Everybody's Magazine, January-June 1903*)

Thomas, William I., and Thomas, Dorothy S., *The Child in America* (Knopf, 1928)

BIBLIOGRAPHY

Thrasher, Frederic M., *The Gang* (University of Chicago, 1927)

Time (*January 15, 1934*)

Union Gospel News (*March 28, 1895*)

Weybright, Victor, "Jane Addams, the Tireless, at Seventy" (*New York Times Magazine, August 31, 1930*)

Wilson, Howard E., *Mary McDowell, Neighbor* (University of Chicago, 1928)

Woods, Robert A., and Kennedy, Albert J., *The Settlement Horizon* (Russell Sage Foundation, 1922)